The Indian National Flag unfurled through Philately

The Indian National Flag unfurled through Philately

Sekhar Chakrabarti

NIYOGI BOOKS

Published by

NIYOGI BOOKS

D-78, Okhla Industrial Area, Phase-I
New Delhi-110 020, INDIA
Tel: 91-11-26816301, 49327000
Fax: 91-11-26810483, 26813830
Email: niyogibooks@gmail.com
Website: www.niyogibooks.com

Editor: Sucharita Ghosh/Niyogi Books
Design: Nabanita Das/Niyogi Books

ISBN: 978-93-81523-39-1
Year of Publication: 2012

Printed at: Niyogi Offset Pvt. Ltd., New Delhi, India

This book is dedicated to the past, present and future generations of our great nation.

Contents

Foreword 9
Preface 13
Abbreviations & Glossary of Terms 15

Flags in Indian Epics and Legends 17
Age of Discovery and Arrival of the European Flags in India 20
Flags of Early Indian Rulers 34
Quest for a Distinctive Pan-Indian Flag 39
Birth of the *Swaraj* Flag 50
Conflicts around the *Swaraj* Flag 60
The *Purna Swaraj* Flag 71
Free India's National Flag 81
Famous Flag-Related Events 102
Uses of Flags: International Forums 107
Flags at Sea 121
Military Flags 126
Legal Aspects, Etiquettes and Protocols 129
Patriotic Songs: Legacy of the Flag Continues 135

Appendices
Appendix-I 'The *Vajra* as a National Flag' by Sister Nivedita, 1909 139
Appendix-II 'The National Flag' by M.K. Gandhi, 1921 144
Appendix-III 'The National Flag' by Prof. Suniti Kumar Chatterji, 1931 146

For Further Reading 155

Index 157

Foreword

Archaeological evidence, going back to 4000 BC, suggests that the Egyptian ships carried a standard consisting of a pole with a totemistic figure at the top. It is generally believed that such a standard was the sign of the province where the ship had been registered. Reference in this connection had been made to the curved ibis emblem atop a pole representing the Ibis province. These totemistic emblems may be the precursor of later-day flags but these were not flags in the sense we understand them.

By 500 BC, the Chinese devised their silk flags of which the dragon flag was most popular. The Parthians of Central Asia adopted the dragon flag model from the Chinese only to transmit it to the Romans who gave it a cylindrical shape. The eagle motif of the Roman empire called *vexillum* (the Latin word for flag) came into use in about the year 100 BC.

All these are known facts of history but what is less known is that the concept of a flag had already been developed in India when the great Bharata war, as told by the *Mahabharata*, was fought between the Kuru and Pandava tribes, not later than 800 BC. While narrating this inter-tribal war, the *Mahabharata* says that the presence of the Pandava hero, Arjuna, in the battlefield could be recognised from the *kapidhvaja* (flag charged with a monkey emblem) fluttering on his war chariot. This flag was also known as *kapiketana, ketana* meaning flag. For this distinctive flag Arjuna was known both as *Kapidhvaja* and *Kapiketana.* By way of commemorating the Bhagavad Gita, India Post released a stamp in 1978, depicting a swallow-tailed *kapidhvaja* on the war chariot of Arjuna. We are not certain whether the *kapidhvaja* was swallow-tailed like European war flags or the monkey on the emblem was in the act of flying in the sky like the *Ramayana* hero Hanuman (the great monkey follower of Rama, the prince of Ayodhya). At least there is no textual support in favour of this design. Another war flag, mentioned by the great epic, is the *makaradhvaja* (flag with a mythical aquatic animal on it). Much later, reference to this flag occurs in the *Raghuvamsa* (c. fifth century) of Kalidasa.

The history of flags in India may be traced even before the time of the *Mahabharata.* The word *ketu* mentioned in the *Rig Veda*, a text datable during a period before 1000 BC, is taken by the Vedic scholars to stand for 'flag'. Indeed *ketana*, that is flag, is a derivative of *ketu.*

In the domain of flags, those with religious affiliation occupy a place of importance. Some such flags, mentioned in the *Mahabharata*, include *makardhvaja* and *vrishadhvaja.* The present-day practice of hoisting a triangular flag on a temple, such as Gurudwara Bodi Sahib temple at Amritsar, may have been a continuation of the older tradition. In Gujarat and Rajasthan, the temple tower had near its peak a projected slab with a socket for holding the flagstaff. At times, these projections were fashioned like a human being with hands holding the shaft of the flag. Such figures were known as *dhvajapurushas.* Hoisting the flag on a temple by a devotee for earning religious merit is an age-old convention. There are persons who charge the devotee a fee for climbing a temple top to erect a flag on the flagstaff. The Lingaraja temple at Bhubaneswar and the Jagannath temple at Puri are two such examples of temples on which professional climbers hoist flags on behalf of the donors.

For flags to be seen from a long distance, sometimes palm trees were made to serve as flagstaffs. This explains why in native lexicons palm trees are called *dhvajavrikshas.* Flags when not in use, were stored in a separate room, which the *Harivamsa* refers to as *dhvajagriha.* It reminds us of *tajiaghars* in the Imambaras where poles upholding *panjas* (metallic hand palms with five fingers symbolising the Prophet Muhammad, his daughter Fatima, her husband Ali and their two sons, Hassan and Hussein) are kept.

The abuse of flags for expressing contempt and hatred for the enemy is a common occurrence. A memorable example is the dishonouring of the swastika and eagle flags introduced by Adolf Hitler after the collapse of Nazi Germany. 'The Victory over Fascism Parade' with plundered Nazi flags at Red Square in Moscow was commemorated by Malagasy by issuing a 100 franc stamp in 1995. Russia released in the following year a 1000 R. stamp bearing M. Mikkhailov's famous painting titled *Laying down of (Nazi) banner*. Interestingly, the plundering of flags (*dhvajahrita*) in a war as a sign of humiliating the enemy was a practice not uncommon in ancient India. When the major part of India was brought under the domination of the Delhi sultans and their commanders, who took little time to transform the newly-conquered territories into independent provinces, flag designs were apparently made to conform to the social and religious affiliation of the conquerors. If this be a fact, not much is known about their flags. It is, however, known that Babur, after putting an end to the Delhi sultanate and founding the Mughal empire in its place, introduced his own flag as an assertion of his supremacy over the conquered land. The flag of Babur is displayed on a stamp of 30 lira denomination released by Turkey in 1987.

All the flags of India, whether ancient or medieval, were either personal or social or religious. The concept of a national flag took a long time to develop. During the sixteenth century, the need for a national flag was felt by the European explorers who began to venture outside their coastal waters. National flags were evolved for ready identification of the ships carrying those explorers. In India, the spirit of nationalism grew only after the British colonial rulers united the country under an alien sovereign. This development generated a sense of nationalism among the Indians to whom foreign domination was not acceptable. The discovery of national identity was followed by the struggle for India's freedom from colonial rule. The search for a national flag was its natural consequence. The result was the birth of the tricolour.

The foregoing is a very brief account of the history of flags in India which evidently suffers from many gaps and unanswered issues. To reconstruct this history is a desideratum. As yet no one has engaged oneself in a painstaking research for meeting this demand. Under the circumstances, it is no little wonder that Mr Sekhar Chakrabarti, an acclaimed philatelist, has taken upon himself the challenging task of narrating the history of Indian flags from the days of yore, deriving information from an unconventional source. It is like the bow of Ulysses which could not be drawn by any weaker hand. He weaves the colourful history of Indian flags gathering data primarily from philatelic materials. The successful completion of this daring venture earns for Mr Chakrabarti a permanent niche in the world of historians engaged in vexillological research.

Dipak Ranjan Das
Former Professor & Head, Department of Ancient History & Culture, Calcutta University

Member: West Bengal Heritage Commission

Preface

Every country has adopted symbols for its flags, coins, currency notes, postage stamps, official stationery, military uniforms and medals, etc. Affirmation of the values of the nation is inherent in the uses of all such symbols. However, the national flag is the strongest and most independent of all symbols. It is an explicit and clear outward expression of how a country sees itself. Today, there is no country in the world which does not have a national flag. A national flag is something more than a mere coloured bunting of which it is made. It incarnates something spiritual. It embodies aspirations and hopes for the future. Intrinsically a flag may be valueless but extrinsically a national flag is priceless. In most countries, people feel that the national flag belongs to the citizens and, therefore, they articulate this by waving it in innumerable social settings which manifest the existence and glorification of the country. Nowadays, it has become a trend to wave the flag colours profusely to cheer their favourite teams in the Olympics and other international sports events. The younger generation is buoyant, overtly or covertly wearing the national colours as facial make-up or waving the flag in all imaginable shapes and sizes. Perhaps, these practices are more honoured in the breach of the respective flag codes than in its observance. Flags motivate people to do things. In the past century and during India's struggle for freedom, many flags were evolved to instil nationalism. Many such historical flags played influential roles and gained the status of the national flag for the whole of India. The history of India's national flag is therefore the history of India's trials and tribulations, sorrows and sacrifices, and the vision to build a better nation.

Postage stamps are tiny works of art, filled with a huge amount of information. They are eloquent ambassadors pronouncing visually the heritage and history far better than only words. The images of flags on stamps and postmarks and postal stationery function as little windows into the past. Commemorative stamps are issued to mark either outstanding events and memorable dates or jubilees of eminent persons or in celebration of a significant achievement. Many such stamps convey authentic information about flags with interesting facsimiles.

The idea of presenting the history of the Indian national flag through philately may therefore be considered a maiden attempt to present accurately and completely the various aspects of India's national flag—its link with the ancient past, and its direct relation with the thought processes that it had represented during various stages of nation-building. The following pages of this book bring alive the history of India's national flag, flag-related events and flag-related personalities through stamps and other collectibles. It is a visual narrative of the story of the flag, stretching from the ancient past to the present, mostly with philatelic illustrations sourced from my lifelong collections.

I have had help from so many people, including foreign embassies and diplomatic sources and fellow collectors. I recall my contact with Dr Whitney Smith, the foremost American flag expert and 'father' of the international vexillological movement. The word 'vexillology' was coined by him in 1958. I am extremely conscious of the support and encouragement received from historian P.T. Nair, Prof. D.R. Das and Dr. M. Kaukub. I am obliged to fellow philatelists Moloy Sarkar, Gopal Biswas, J. Bareira, Kenneth Sequeira, Cdr. U.N. Acharya, I.N. (Rtd), and D. Hemchandra Rao for harnessing information and for permitting me to use Philatelic material from their collections. I am thankful to Pritha Chakrabarty and Suvra Chakrabarti Roy for preparing the basic text and to Saumya Chakrabarti for selection of the illustrations. To Tultul Niyogi, who for the first time came up with the idea of publishing this book, I extend my gratitude. Many thanks to Sucharita Ghosh for editing this book with meticulous care and to Nabanita Das for her diligent efforts in designing. I hope that everybody to whom I am indebted, including my wife Sukla Chakrabarti, for their unstinted support, will accept my grateful thanks for all they have done.

Abbreviations & Glossary of Terms

AICC	All India Congress Committee.
Bunting	A traditional woollen fabric used for making flags. Indian national flags for official use are made of cotton-khadi cloth. Terry-cotton is the proper fabric for manufacture of naval flags at sea.
Cachet	A printed or rubber-stamped inscription or illustration added to an envelope to publicise an event or anniversary.
Cancellation	Defacement made by postal authorities primarily for the purpose of preventing re-use of a postage stamp.
Canton	A square or rectangular section of a flag usually in the upper left corner next to the staff.
Charge	Any figure, symbol or emblem placed on a flag.
Coat of arms	Emblems and figures forming the symbolic insignia of a nation. The main elements of a coat of arms are the shield, the crest, wreath, helmet, supporters, compartments and motto.
Cinderella	Stamp-like label which is not valid for international postage.
Commemorative	Stamp issued to mark an important event or anniversary and usually on sale for a limited period.
CWC	Congress Working Committee.
Duplex	Postmark in two sections: a circular date-stamp and a pattern/device alongside.
EIC	East India Company.
Ensign	A flag used to indicate the nationality of civil, government and naval ships. Ensign is flown by ships at or near the stern.

Essay An 'essay' is a printed design proposed for a stamp but not adopted as proposed.

FDC First Day Cover; an envelope bearing new stamps postmarked on the day they are issued.

Field The background colour of a flag.

INC Indian National Congress.

Jack A flag flown at the bow of a warship, indicating nationality.

Maximum Card Pictorial postcard, duplicating the design of a stamp, with the stamp affixed to the pictorial side and cancelled with a postal marking relating to the picture.

Miniature Sheet A souvenir specially printed, and usually with wide margins specially inscribed, containing one or a small number of postage stamps, issued to commemorate some event.

Philately Systematic study of postage stamps, postmarks, postal stationery and similar items. The word, coined by Georges Herpin in 1864, is formed by two Greek words: *'phileo'* meaning 'I love' and *'ateleia'* meaning 'exemption from payment'.

Postal Stationery Pre-paid postal items such as envelopes, aerogrammes and postcards on which postage stamps are printed.

Se-tenant Stamps of different designs, colours or face values printed on the same sheet.

Sheet Watermarks Watermarks incorporated in sheets of paper upon which stamps are printed so that the device, officially required, appears only once in the sheet, extending more or less throughout the area of the paper.

Specimen The overprint applied to stamps intended as samples.

'Sun in its splendour' When a sun bears a human face and is surrounded by rays.

Vexillology Scholarly study of all aspects of flags. *'Vexillum'* being the Latin word for flag and *'-logy'* being the Greek suffix for study.

Flags in Indian Epics and Legends

The earliest flags and standards were almost always of a religious nature, either sacred symbols to be worshipped, or an emblem which indicated or promoted communication with the gods, and the authority of a flag or standard was initially derived from the power of these religious connexions ...[1]

In early days, flags were solid objects or standards set on poles. The modern flag's ancestral roots lie in the standards of rulers, armies and religious leaders of the ancient oriental civilisations.

The earliest reference to flags was found in the sacred Hindu scriptures—the Vedas. In the *Rig Vedas*, written in about 5000 BC, the flag was described as *'ketu'* (banner). In *Atharva Veda* two lines clearly indicate a common flag with a symbol of *Surya* or the Sun God for the Aryans. As time advanced and Aryans came to settle in different areas conquered by them, they had to resort to different badges and emblems of distinguishing marks. In the ancient Indian literatures and epics, the *Ramayana* and the *Mahabharata,* roughly dating between fifth to fourth century BC, we see a large number of kings and princes each with a distinctive *dhvaja* (standard) or *ketu* decorated with a particular *rupa-lakshma* (symbol) assigned from an object or animal figure. There are long lists devoted to the description of *dhvajas* of the heroes of *Mahabharata* in the *Drona Parva* (80.1-29). Images of the hanuman or monkey, the lion, the bull, the peacock, the bear, the elephant, the serpent and the eagle were prominent among fauna that were selected as the symbols displayed on the flags. There were other art forms depicting *dhvajas*, such as, sculptures carved on top of *stamvas* or pillars,

①

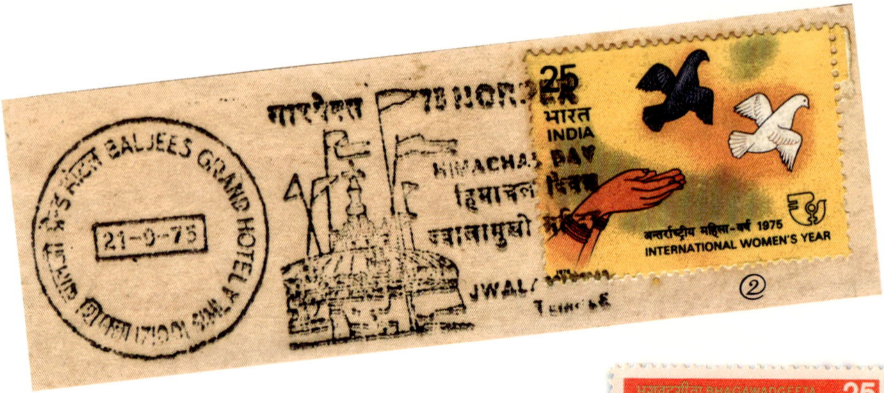

②

known as *dhvaja stamvas.* The association of a pillar or a *dhvaja* with a religious shrine was a very ancient feature.

③

The 25-paisa stamp issued in 1978 to commemorate the Bhagavad Gita, the ancient Hindu scripture, depicts Arjuna's *dhvaja*, a swallow-tailed flag fluttering on his war chariot, in the 'Battle of Kurukshetra' fought between the Pandavas and the Kauravas. The *dhvaja* had the figure of *Maha-Kapi* or Monkey God, having the unique feature of a *simha-langula*, which means the tail of a lion.

Triangular pieces of fabric fastened to the top of a pole were popular in ancient India. These flags were essentially religious in nature and were treated as devices for communication with the gods.

In many Indian temples there are a great many flags decorated with the Sanskrit representation of the sacred sound ॐ or 'Aum', taken from *Mandukya Upanishad.* The sound ॐ is composed of English equivalents 'A + U + M', where 'A' signifies *apti* or attaining, common to all wakeful humans; 'U' denotes *utkarsha* or uprising from mundane objects to subtle elements, as in a dream state; 'M' connotes *miti* or measure, its root meaning 'to end' the waking state and attain sleep. Once integrated, these sounds form the supreme sound ॐ which transcends all other states. It means the Ultimate, the all pervading Atman or soul.

The evolution of Dravidian civilisation and culture in South India was centered around ancient Madurai, the capital of the 2500-years-old Pandyan kingdom. The emblem of the Pandya dynasty was *meen* or fish.

④

⑤

The Pandyan king is sometimes referred to as *Meenavan* or *Mathsyaraja*. Their deity was goddess *Meenatchi*. The name *'Meenatchi'* suggests one who rules over the Pandyan dynasty. Pandyans ruled Madurai till as late as the fourteenth century.

The imperial Guptas (AD fourth century) were devotees of Lord Vishnu and had adopted *Garuda dhvaja* as their standard. They had erected several *Garuda*-topped pillars that were dedicated to Lord Vishnu.

① *Stamp of the Vedas, issued by Mauritius.*

② *The postmark depicts triangular flags atop a temple.*

③ *25-paisa stamp issued in 1978 to commemorate the Bhagavad Gita.*

④ *The pictorial postmark of Madurai Philatelic Bureau shows the Pandyan flag depicting the emblem of* meen *or fish.*

⑤ *Gold coin of Chandragupta I. The coin shows Chandragupta offering oblations with his right hand on the altar of* Garuda dhvaja.

Endnote:

1. Terence Wise, *Military Flags of the World* (Poole, Dorset: Blandford Press Ltd., 1977), p. 25.

Age of Discovery and Arrival of the European Flags in India

During the 'Age of Discovery', a period between early fifteenth century and early seventeenth century, exploration of maritime routes to India for trade became an influential activity of several European powers, which was encouraged by the famed riches of India and more specifically for exotic spices and textiles. For the Europeans, the search for an alternative sea route was essential to sidestep the Arabian merchants who controlled the prevalent caravan routes through the deserts in the Middle East. With such expeditions and discoveries, flags of the European powers with different designs reached faraway shores,

(1)

including India. The Age of Discovery saw the development of heraldic sails usually painted with armorial devices all over, besides banners and pennons of expeditions flown from the top of the ships' masts. The dramatic changes during this age in the designs of flags at sea, with devices symbolic of a particular nationality, ultimately gave way to many a present-day national flags of the world.

The sea route from Europe to the Indian Ocean via the Cape of Good Hope in South Africa was pioneered by the Portuguese explorer Vasco da Gama in 1498, resulting in the establishment of new maritime routes for trade. Perhaps, it was also the beginning of European colonialism in India.

The Portuguese voyages of exploration were inspired by Henry the Navigator, who was grand master of the 'Order of Christ'. The 'Flag of the Order' was used extensively by Portuguese explorers. It was in the memory of Henry the Navigator that the armilla or armillary sphere was used in later Portuguese flags.[1]

Description printed on the gumside of the stamp (see illustration 3) in Portuguese, French and English reads: 'A composition with Hindu elements' on the portrait of Vasco da Gama hanging in the Sociedade de Geografia in Lisbon, Portugal.

The world's first 'Omnibus Issue', which was a set of eight stamps in as many different designs, was issued on 1 April 1898 from Portugal and its overseas colonies, including *Estado da Índia* or Portuguese India, on the occasion of the four hundredth anniversary of the 'discovery of sea route to India' by Vasco da Gama.

②

③

④

① Miniature sheet released in 1998 by Portugal to commemorate the 500th anniversary of Vasco da Gama's discovery of the sea route to India.

② Henry the Navigator.

③ Vasco da Gama.

④ Current national flag of Portugal.

⑤

⑥

⑦

⑧

Portuguese India or Goa as it is known today, was established in 1505, seven years after Vasco da Gama's discovery of the sea route to India. Portuguese India comprised a number of enclaves on India's western coast, including Goa proper, the coastal enclaves of Daman (Damao) and Diu, and the enclaves of Dadra and Nagar Haveli. After India gained independence from the British in 1947, Portugal refused to accede to India's demand to relinquish their control of its territories. *Times of India,* on 11 June 1947, published a statement made on the previous day in Lisbon by Captain Teofilo Duarte, the then Portuguese minister of colonies, under the caption 'Portugal will not quit': 'The Portuguese flag will not fall down in India without some thousands of Portuguese white and coloured, shedding their blood in its defence.' The enclaves of Dadra and Nagar Haveli were annexed to India in 1954, and the remaining territories were liberated from Portugal in December 1961. Portugal recognised the annexation in 1975. The Portuguese state flag which was adopted and used since 1911 was replaced by the Indian national flag on the day of liberation of Goa on 19 December 1961.

European flags at sea with colonial ambitions

Ab initio, there was no international trade without conflict. After the decisive English victory over the Spanish Armada in 1588, the sea trade monopolies of the Portuguese in the East and the Spanish in the West Indies fell into rough waters within a century. Trade rivalries brought the other European powers to India in the early seventeenth century. The Dutch, British, French and Danes, one after the other, followed suit and established trading posts in different coastal areas of India. All of them carried their distinctive maritime ensigns and banners of their rulers to proclaim initial trading rights and subsequent strategic territorial rights.

⑨

⑤ Cartiografia Portuguesa: Carta do atlas de lopo Homem-Reines, *1519(Portuguese Cartography by Lopo Homem-Reines, 1519.) The maximum card issued by Portugal in 1997 is seen decorated with sixteenth-century Portuguese flags at sea.*

⑥, ⑦ *Arrival of Vasco da Gama's fleet at Calicut.*

⑧ *Liberation of Goa.*

⑨ *Seventeenth-century European flags at sea with colonial ambitions (clockwise from top: British, French, Portuguese, Dutch and Spanish).*

Arrival of the Dutch Tricolour

The *Vereenigde Oostindische Compagnie* (VOC), quite literally the Dutch East India Company or the United East Indian Company was a chartered company formed in 1602. The Dutch colonial possessions in the Indian subcontinent survived between 1605 and 1818.

The red, white and blue flag, composed of three horizontal bands, has been the national flag of the Netherlands since the seventeenth century. The colours of the flag were based on the livery of Prince William I of Orange-Nassau, the founder of the Dutch Royal House.

⑪⑫

⑪⑫ *The Dutch East India Company ensign with the letters VOC inscribed on the Dutch national flag.*

The Battle of Colachel (Kulachal, Tamil Nadu) was fought in July 1741 between forces of the erstwhile kingdom of Travancore and the Dutch East India Company. The Dutch marines under the leadership of a Flemish naval commander, Captain Eustachius De Lannoy (D'lennoy), were sent to Travancore to secure a trading post from the Maharaja Marthanda Varma. They landed

11

with artillery at Kulachal, and captured the territory upto Padmanabhapuram (the capital of erstwhile Travancore). But soon thereafter, the Raja's army defeated the Dutch. It was the first major defeat of a European military force by someone from South Asia. This victory is commemorated by a pillar erected at the site by the Travancore government (the pillar also appears on the stamp above). It has a conch adorning the top of the pillar and on its base are inscribed the following words: 'In remembrance of all the brave men of Travancore Army who laid down their lives in defeating the superior Dutch forces during the Battle of Colachel in July 1741.'

Arrival of the English Flag

Towards the last phase of Queen Elizabeth I's reign, a royal charter was granted on 31 December 1600 to a joint stock company described as 'The Governor and Company of Merchants of London Trading into the East Indies', popularly known as 'East India Company' or 'John Company'. The East India Company's ship *Hector,* a chartered galleon of the third voyage, arrived at the confluence of Gulf of Cambay of the Arabian Sea and the river Tapti in Surat (formerly known as Suryapur) on 24 August 1608. The *Hector,* commanded by Captain William Hawkins, was the first ship to fly an English flag—the St George's Cross flag in India.[2]

12

The St George's Cross flag—a red cross on a white field, was adopted by England and the city of London in 1190 for their ships to enter the Mediterranean sea. The flag achieved the status of the unofficial national flag of England since at least 1277. Interestingly though, Great Britain does not have any official national flag as yet and has no flag code as such. However, at sea there have evolved strict etiquettes in England regarding the usage of ensigns and the occasions on which they are to be used.

Later, the Red Ensign—a red flag with the red cross of St George on a white canton—was established as the proper colours for British ships sailing

①③

anywhere in the world by a royal proclamation in 1674. However, the East India Company was allowed to have its own special ensign. There is evidence that as far back as 1616 the EIC had a striped ensign with a cross at the canton.[3]

①④

Edward Barlow, an English seaman who made his first voyage to India in 1670, possessed the habit of maintaining a diary and embellished it with coloured sketches. His sketches show ships at Bombay (renamed Mumbai in 1995), Calicut and Surat adorned with flags with red and white stripes and the St George's Cross at the canton. The number of stripes varies from nine to eleven to thirteen. Later he made another voyage and drew more sketches. His later sketches have flags with seven stripes and even one with nineteen stripes. Barlow's paintings suggest that in addition to the East India Company's flag, the ships carried a red ensign with the Cross of St George on a white canton.[4]

On 12 April 1606, a Royal Proclamation announced the introduction of the first Union flag

①① Surrender of De Lannoy. Indian Post issued a Rs 5 stamp on 1 April 2004 to commemorate the 300th anniversary of the raising of the 9th Battalion of the Madras (Travancore) Regiment.

①② Queen Elizabeth I.

①③ Stamp depicting St George's Cross flag to commemorate 1700th anniversary of St George.

①④ EIC's ensign (c.1616–1707).

combining the St George's Cross of England and St Andrew's diagonal Cross of Scotland. After the legislative union of England and Scotland in 1707, the Union flag substituted the Cross of St George on East India Company's flag.

The Continental Colors or the Grand Union Flag, the first navy ensign (1775–1777) of the United States of America was identical to East India Company's ensign. It combined the first British Union flag of 1606 and the thirteen stripes signifying colonial unity of the thirteen states in USA. George Washington, the first President of the USA chose it to be flown to celebrate the formation of the Continental Army on New Year's day in

15

16

17

18

19

1776. On that day the Grand Union Flag was proudly hailed on Prospect Hill in Somerville, near his headquarters in Cambridge, Massachusetts.

After the union of Great Britain and Ireland in 1800, the red diagonal Cross of St Patrick was added to the existing combination of the Cross of St Andrew and the Cross of St George, to create the new version of the Union Jack. A royal decree, authorising the use of the new Union Jack on the ensign, was issued in 1801, whereby the East India Company was obliged to change its ensign for the third time.

The growing Portuguese influence on Indian soil was checked by the English when they won the decisive naval victory over the Portuguese off the coast of Surat in 1612.

The British, however, settled down in Madras (present-day Chennai) in 1629. In 1640 they built a fort in Madras and named it Fort Saint George.

In 1687, Elihu Yale, the then Governor of Madras state (renamed Tamil Nadu in 1969), after whom the Ivy League Yale University in the USA was named, hoisted the Union Jack for the first time replacing that of the East India Company on the flagstaff at Fort St George in the city of Madras. The three-tier flagstaff, forty-seven and half metres long, the oldest and tallest in India, was originally made of teak, the bottom tier of which came from a ship wrecked off the Madras coast around 1687.

On 15 August 1947, it was on this majestic flag-mast at Fort St George that the Indian tricolour was

25 *East Indiamen wearing the Company's ensigns.* View of Bombay *by Edward Barlow.*

26 *East India Company's ensign (1707–1801).*

27 *East India Company's ensign (1801–1873).*

28 *Grand Union Flag.*

29 *View of Surat from the sea, c. 1670, by Ludolf Bakhuizen (1631–1708).*

20 *Colonel Mark Wilks and view of Fort St George, Madras. The stamp was issued to commemorate the 150th death anniversary of Colonel Mark Wilks by Isle of Man in 1981.*

21 *The pictorial cancellation depicts St George's flag-mast.*

20

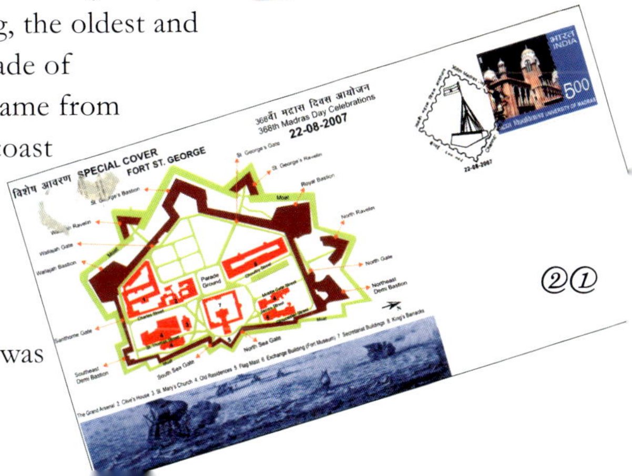

21

hoisted for the first time and since then the national flag has been flying on it. It is also the venue of the annual Independence Day flag-hoisting ceremony in Chennai. The national flag, which was hoisted on 15 August 1947, is preserved in the Fort museum.

Age and the vagaries of weather had taken their toll on the 307-year-old flag-mast and it became too weak despite the two dozen guy-wires supporting it against the gusty breeze from the Bay of Bengal. In 1994, the towering flag-mast, a familiar landmark in the city, was replaced by a metallic one matching the original in size and form.

In 1690 Job Charnock established a factory at Calcutta (renamed Kolkata in 2001). In 1698 the factory was fortified and named Fort William. British rule in India was firmly established in 1757 when the forces of the East India Company defeated the Nawab of Bengal in the Battle of Plassey. However now it has been established that 24 August 1690 was not the birth date of Calcutta, nor was Job Charnock its founder. Calcutta existed long before the arrival of Charnock, at least since the fifteenth century.

22

23

S.S. Hindostan, the British mail ship of P&O line on her maiden voyage from Southampton to Calcutta via Galle (Ceylon / Sri Lanka) in 1842, is depicted in illustrations 23 and 24. The Indian stamp issued in

24

25

26

27

1997 shows the ship flying a Blue Ensign—an incorrect depiction since it was flying a Red Ensign. Also the ship's name is spelled as 'Hindosthan' whereas P&O spelled the name as 'Hindostan'.

Sheet watermarks on paper were created for the purpose of printing the first Indian postage stamps at the surveyor general's office in Calcutta in 1854. The watermark has the East India Company's coat-of-arms amongst other symbols while the British lions are holding St George's Cross flags of England.

28

The first stamps valid for postage throughout India were placed on sale on 1 October 1854 under the authority of the East India Company. The stamps were in four denominations: half anna, one anna, two annas and four annas. They featured a youthful profile of Victoria—Queen of the United Kingdom of Great Britain, crowned Empress of India in 1877. All four values, considered to be classics, were designed and printed in Calcutta. All were lithographed

29

30

22 *View of Calcutta, c. 1690, seen on Rs 6 denomination stamp issued in celebration of Calcutta's tercentenary on 24 August 1990.*

23 *Indian stamp commemorating mail ship* S.S. Hindostan *but with incorrect details.*

24 S.S. Hindostan *depicted on the cover of the 'Story of P&O', 1837–1987.*

25 *Sheet watermarks used for printing the first set of Indian postage stamps, 1854.*

26 *Robert Clive and Mir Jafar after the Battle of Plassey, 1757; oil on canvas by Francis Hayman (1708–1776).*

27 *India's most famous stamp with a major error: inverted head. The four-annas stamp is one of the world's first bicoloured stamps.*

28 *One anna, half anna and two anna stamps: issued by East India Company in 1854 for postage in India.*

29, 30 *Union flag or Union Jack: 1801–to date.*

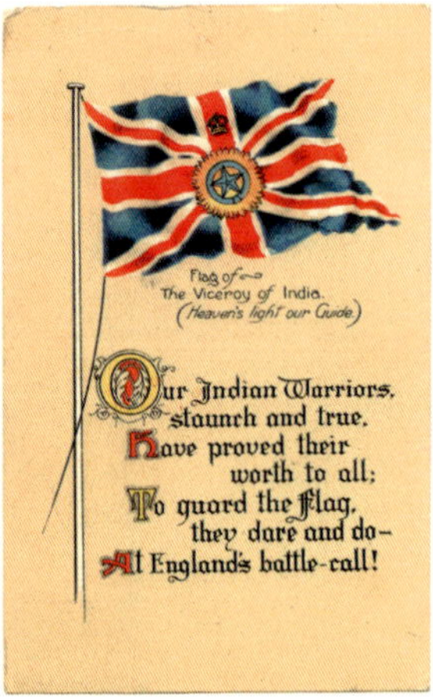

③①

except for the two-annas stamp, which was produced by typography. These were issued without perforations or gum.

Since about 1885 till 1947, the viceroy of India flew a Union flag augmented in the centre with the 'Star of India' and the legend 'Heaven's light our Guide' surmounted by a crown. This flag was also used by the governors, lieutenant governors, chief commissioners and other British officers in India.

On the eve of the coronation of Edward VII in May 1902, perhaps for the first time, William Coldstream, an Englishman and a retired Indian civil service officer sent a letter to the Indian office in London urging the necessity of a distinctive Indian flag. He also wrote, 'It is pertinent to note that the symbolism of a flag is appreciated in India more than in England.'[5]

In June 1911, around the time of the coronation of King George V, King of the United Kingdom and the British Dominions and Emperor of India, Oliver Russell, 2nd Baron Ampthill, former governor of Madras and former acting viceroy of India (from April to December of 1904), strongly advocated the necessity of a common flag for British India, especially when every one of the British colonies owned their own distinctive flags. These efforts, however, bore no fruitful result.

Arrival of the French *Tricolore*

During the reign of King Louis XIV, it was Jean-Baptiste Colbert who in 1664 established *La Compagnie Française des Indes Occidentales* (French East India Company) to compete with rival European powers, viz. the Portuguese, the Dutch and the English in India. The French had begun to visit India since the seventeenth century, amongst whom were the famous travellers, Francois Bernier and Jean Baptiste Travernier. They wrote interesting and valuable accounts about what they perceived to be the hidden treasures and curiosities of India. In 1676, Emperor Aurengzeb gave a *firman* (permission) to the French EIC for doing business and to establish their factories. Unlike British or Dutch Companies, the French EIC, it appears had no distinctive flag of its own. The French EIC's commercial activity rapidly changed after the outbreak of the French Revolution. The French EIC was closed down in 1794 when the French

32

government took charge of all its possessions and assets in India.

Abraham Creques (official map and compass-maker to Peter III of Aragon) made a map (see illustration 32) in 1375, as a gift for the French king. The map shows the section of the kingdom of Delhi, superimposed on an oblique grid of compass bearings for the *Atlas of the world*.[6]

In the past, French kings, officials and regiments all had their own flag or flags, some with long traditions behind them. The French Revolution of 1789 swept the French royal flags of *ancien regime* away and replaced those with the blue, white and red *'Tricolore'*. The *Tricolore* was introduced as the official flag of the French Navy in 1790. It became the national flag of France by a decree passed by the Convention in 1794. After the battle of Waterloo, with the final downfall of Napoleon and the restoration of the Bourbon monarchy, the *Tricolore* was abandoned in favour of the white flag of *émigrés*. However, the Revolution

33

31 *The official British flag for India.*

32 *Kingdom of Delhi depicted on a map by Abraham Creques, 1375.*

33 *The Fleur-de-Lis, the French Royal Flag and Ensign (1643–1790).*

34 *This French military colour defaced by an Indian snake was said to have been carried in the First Maratha War of 1779–1782, a prototype of pre-Revolution French colours, but without the snake.*

34

35

of 1830 brought back the blue, white and red flag. Since 1848 the French *Tricolore* had been in use uninterruptedly.

36

Taking advantage of the dwindling Mughal power, the French began to intervene in Indian political affairs with the ulterior motive of establishing a French empire in India, especially by forging alliances with local rulers in south India. From 1741 the French, under Joshep Francois Dupleix, who in 1742 was elevated as Governor General of French India, pursued a hostile policy against both the Indians and the British until they were ultimately defeated by the growing British forces.

During the Anglo-French Wars, the French lost most of their territories in India. The French *Tricolore* remained visible only in French settlements of Chandernagor in the state of West Bengal and Pondicherry.

37

When India became independent on 15 August 1947, Chandernagor was required to choose its political destiny. The French declared Chandernagor to be a *Ville Libre* (free city) on 27 November 1947 and constituted an administrative council consisting of the people of Chandernagor. The *de jure* transfer of Chandernagor to the Indian Union took place on 9 June 1952.

38

Pondicherry, fondly called *La Côte d'Azur de l'Est* (French Riviera of the East) was merged with independent India in 1954 and renamed Puducherry (later).

Worldwide impact of the French *Tricolore*

The *Tricolore* made a massive impact on politically-minded people throughout the world. Before the French Revolution, it was the monarchy and not the people who had a flag. The French *Tricolore* in large part created the contemporary sense of people's participation in the formation of the nation state which we take for granted nowadays. The French *Tricolore*

③⑨

inspired revolutionaries and leaders of the radical or independence movements in all parts of the world. It was, therefore, not surprising that attempts were made in several countries to imitate the *Tricolore*. Inspired by the French *Tricolore*, India's first flag was devised, which was hoisted in Calcutta on the Boycott Day in 1906 to protest against the partition of Bengal. Flags with three vertical bands were adopted by revolutionary movements in Mexico. The tricolour design was prescribed by Napoleon for adoption by Italy. The national flag of Haiti is derived from the *Tricolore* after Haiti freed herself from French Occupation in 1804. Hungary, Ireland, Belgium, Norway, Romania, Costa Rica, the Dominican Republic and many other aspiring nations, including former French colonies in Africa, adopted their respective national flags by replicating the French *Tricolore*.

③⑤ *Dupleix meeting the Soudhabar of the Deccan (c. 1750), by Alphonse-Marie-Adolphe de Neuville (1835–1885).*

③⑥ *A typical military colours of the French Corps in the service of Tipu Sultan in the campaign of 1792.*

③⑦ *Seal of Chandernagor Administrative council, set up by the French.*

③⑧ *De-facto transfer of Pondicherry.*

③⑨ *Stamp depicting the French national flag issued by United Nations.*

Endnotes:

1. C. William, *The World of Flags* (London: Studio Editions, 1990), p.118.
2. Philip Mason, *The Men Who Ruled India* (New Delhi: Rupa & Co, 1992), p. 4.
3. W. Rea Furlong and B. McCandless, *So Proudly We Hail* (Washington: Smithsonian Institution Press, 1981), p. 43.
4. Ibid.
5. Arundhati Virmani, *A National Flag for India* (Ranikhet: Permanent Black, 2008), pp. 12–13.
6. Photograph courtesy of the Bibliotheque Nationale, Paris.

①

Flags of Early Indian Rulers

Previously, every independent kingdom in India had its own distinctive flag or banner that signified the pride and power of those kingdoms and their rulers.

Shivaji Bhosle (1630–1680), also known as Chhatrapati Shivaji, after his successful military campaigns against the Mughals adopted the *bhagyazenda* (saffron flag) of his guru Ramdas. It was a *zuri-pataka*—a swallow-tailed flag made by joining two triangular-shaped flags. It became the symbol of the Hindu Maratha Empire. Chhatrapati Shivaji led a resistance to free the Marathas from the sultanate of Bijapur, and established the rule of the *'Hindavi Swarajya'* or a sovereign Hindu state. He created an independent Maratha kingdom with Raigad as its capital in present-day Maharashtra in 1674.

Inspired by Harry Arbuthnot Acworth's 'Ballads of Marathas', Rabindranath Tagore composed his famous poem *'Pratinidhi'* or 'Representative'.[1] In *'Pratinidhi'* Tagore reasserts, 'Shivaji had adopted his saffron flag in consonance with the spirit of renunciation as symbolised by the saffron scarf of the mendicants and the ascetics, following a desire expressed to him by his religious mentor Guru Ramdas.'

②

Shivaji founded a formidable navy in the seventeenth century. The *'Pal'* and the *'Galbat'*, the two

③

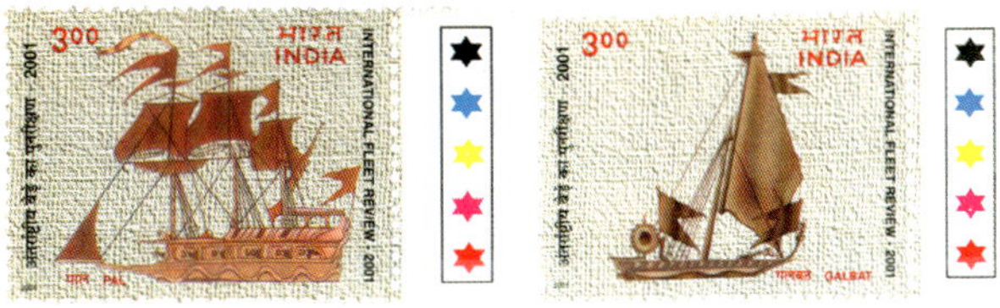

types of warships, bearing the *zuri-pataka,* had participated in the fleet reviews of the Maratha navy off the coast of Ratnagiri upon the Arabian Sea. The ships depicted on the stamps (see illustration 3) are from the paintings of ships from the Maratha period (c. eighteenth century).

④

The legendary *Gandabherunda* possessing two heads each, facing away from the other, was the emblem of the Mysore rulers of the Wodeyar dynasty. They first ruled Mysore c. 1399 to 1796 and again from 1799 to 1950.

⑤

Standards of Islamic rulers of Mysore (1761–1799) were carried before Sultan Hyder Ali and his son and heir Tipu Sultan, the 'Tiger of Mysore'.

Tipu Sultan adopted the tiger and the sun as his emblems. According to Sufi traditions, the sun represents the source of divine light. These banners were captured by the British at the Siege of Srirangapatnam (now Seringapatnam) in 1799.

Following the defeat and death of Tipu Sultan in 1799, his family was held captive at Vellore Fort. In July 1806, when the Indian soldiers at Vellore

⑥

① *'Chatrapati Shivaji' cancellation applied on the FDC commemorating Shivaji.*

② *Guru Samarth Ramdas.*

③ *Indian stamps portraying ships inspired by eighteenth-century Maratha paintings.*

④ Gandabherunda: *emblem of the Mysore rulers of Wodeyar dynasty.*

⑤ *Tipu Sultan.*

⑥ *Lord Cornwallis receiving Tipu Sultan's sons as hostages (c. 1793). Painting by Robert Home (1752–1834) exhibited at the Royal Academy, 1797.*

rose in revolt against the British, they raised the 'Royal Tiger flag' of Tipu Sultan over Vellore Fort, after pulling down the British Union Jack. However, the uprising was short-lived and suppressed

⑦ immediately by the British when reinforcements arrived.

Maharaja Ranjit Singh fought against his opponents in all encounters under the Sikh golden-yellow banner, the *Nishan Saheb,* bearing the Sikh emblem *Khanda Kirpan,* made up of a solid circle, two interlocked swords and a double-edged sword in black.

The Ranas of Chittor claimed descent from the *Surya Vansi* or Sun Dynasty. They carried a triangular *nishan* (flag) bearing a 'sun in its splendour' on the crimson field called *'Changi'*. The flag bore a *katar* (a type of dagger)—a symbol of independence for the defender of Hinduism.

⑧

⑨

⑩

(11)

(12)

Rani Lakshmi Bai flew her 'Hanuman *jhanda*' (Hanuman flag) during the campaign against the British. It was a triangular flag made of silk, woven with gold threads and studded with precious stones. Lakshmi Bai's flag, with the picture of a hanuman holding a mountain on his left palm, was captured by the British in 1857. The captured flag was in the possession of Unit 5 of the Rajputana Rifles. In 1977 it was dispatched to the Rifles Regimental Centre at the Delhi Cantonment. When Unit 5 of the Rajputana Rifles requested it be returned in 1980, it was found missing. All investigations thereafter failed to trace the flag. *Times of India* on 11 April 1992 reported that the case, which was subsequently conducted by the Central Bureau of Investigation (CBI), was finally closed in 1992 when inquiries made through Interpol and Indian embassies abroad also failed to provide any clue.

(7) *Stamp commemorating the Vellore Mutiny, 1806.*

(8) *The special cover and postmark from Lahore issued on 10 February 2007, commemorates 200 years of Conquest of Kasur by Maharaja Ranjit Singh in 1807.*

(9), (10) *The* Pancha Ranga *was the state standard of Jaipur. The name had its origin in the five horizontal stripes of salmon-pink, white, red, yellow and green.*

(11) *Stamps commemorating First War of Independence, 1857.*

(12) *Lakshmi Bai, Queen of Jhansi (1835–1858).*

During the First War of Independence, Abu Zafar Sirajuddin Muhammad Bahadur Shah Zafar, better known as Bahadur Shah II (1775–1862), the last Mughal Emperor of India, had adopted the lotus flower and the chapatti on a green and gold field as his standard.

Hindu, Mussalman, Sikh hamara
Bhai-bhai pyara
Yeh hai jhanda azadi-ka
Ise salaam hamara.[2]

(Hindu, Mussalman, Sikh are all our dear brothers
This is the flag of our freedom. We salute it.)

Bahadur Shah Zafar

Endnotes:

1. Rabindranath Tagore, *'Katha'* in *Rabindra Rachanabali*, vol. iv (Calcutta: Visva Bharati Publishing Department, 1986), p. 21.
2. Lt Cdr K.V. Singh, *Our National Flag* (New Delhi: Publications Division, 1991), p.19.

Quest for a Distinctive Pan-Indian Flag

National Professor Suniti Kumar Chatterji wrote in 1931,

> There is no ancient flag or banner whether of Hindu or Muhammadan times, which we can think of for adoption as the flag of our country as a whole. Imperial or local princely houses had their standards, e.g. the *Garuda* Standard of the Imperial Guptas. But even when nearly the whole of India was united under the Mauryas in the 3rd century B.C. and the Moguls in the 17th century A.C. no *national* flag or crest seems to have been thought of. India was never physically a *nation militante*, and so there was no need of a national symbol to rally round, in opposition to other nations. Besides, the *political* unity of India that we are now conscious of was an entirely new thing.’[1]

①

②

In the late nineteenth century, when the national leaders in India became passionately infused with the spirit of reasserting the country's independence, they felt the need for a distinctive national flag for India as a whole. There were many tentative essays about flag making.

In the French *Tricolore* Raja Rammohun Roy (1772–1833) perhaps saw the dream of India's independence. During his voyage to England on board *S.S. Albion* in January 1831, seeing two French frigates anchored at Table Bay, Cape Town wearing the French revolutionary *Tricolore*, he insisted on visiting them. The sight of these colours seemed to kindle the flame of his enthusiasm. He was conducted over the vessels and endeavoured to convey through the aid of interpreters what a delight it was to be under the banner that waved over their decks. He proclaimed it be an evidence of the glorious triumph of right over might and as he left the vessels he repeated emphatically, 'Glory, glory, glory to France!'[2]

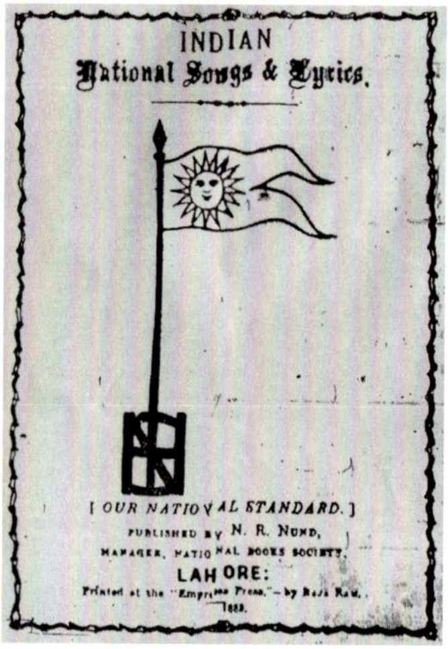
INDIAN
National Songs & Lyrics.

[OUR NATIONAL STANDARD.]
PUBLISHED BY N. R. NUND,
MANAGER, NATIONAL BOOKS SOCIETY,
LAHORE:
Printed at the "Empress Press," — by Raja Ram,
1883.

③

Is there no hope, is there no scope
For freedom's friendly strife?
From Ripon's hand, and old England
Sure justice will arrive.[3]

In 1883 the Indian National Society (INS) was established in Lahore in present-day Pakistan. The moving spirit was Sris Chandra Basu, the founder of Panini Office. Basu became completely involved in all the nationalist and socialist movements in Lahore. He created a national standard—a traditional swallow-tailed flag charged with a 'sun in its splendour'. The flag was paraded through the streets of Lahore by the members of the INS. The facsimile of the national standard was printed above the caption 'Our National Standard' on the title page of *Indian National Songs and Lyrics* written by Basu himself and published by the Society in 1883.

Lotus as a national symbol

One who performs his duty without attachment, surrendering the results unto the Supreme Lord, is unaffected by sinful action, as the lotus is untouched by water.[4]

It was perhaps Rajnarain Bose (1826–1899) who first suggested the lotus as a national symbol in his book *Bridhya Hindoo-r Asha* (An Old Hindoo's Desire) written in 1888, inspired by an article published in the English daily *The Liberal.* Rajnarain Bose was also known as *'Jatiya Bhaber Udbodhak'* (the creator of the national spirit). The lotus is India's ancient symbol of divine beauty, fertility and purity. It is one of the *vajrayana astamangala*, symbolising creation and cosmic regeneration. In the *chakra* and *mandala* it suggests the symbolism of the *dharmachakra.* The lotus is associated with Hindu gods and goddesses and later evoked by Buddhists, Jains and Hindus alike. In Buddhism the lotus symbolises the purity of body, speech and mind. It is also representative of detachment because drops of water slip easily off its petals. The four elements—earth, air, fire and water—are emblematically united in the lotus. The roots deep in the earth grow because of water. Air nurtures its leaves, and it comes to bloom through the force of the fiery sun.

Sister Nivedita's *Vajra* flag, 1904

The first serious attempt at flag-making came from Sister Nivedita (1867–1911), an Irish devotee of Swami Vivekananda. Born as Margaret Elizabeth Nobel in Northern Ireland, she met Swami Vivekananda in London in 1895. Swami Vivekananda inspired her to come to Calcutta to spread education among Indian women. She was given the name Nivedita, meaning the Dedicated One. Sister Nivedita actively participated in the *Swadeshi* movement, a political movement to attain self-sufficiency, and greatly contributed towards Indian nationalism. Sister Nivedita conceived the idea of the national flag during a visit to Bodh Gaya in 1904, in the company of Jagadish Chandra Bose and Rabindranath Tagore. She was inspired by the *vajra* (thunderbolt) sign, a symbol of Buddha, that implies 'the selfless man'. It was the weapon of Lord Indra and is a symbol of strength. It is also associated with the Goddess

④

⑤

① *Raja Rammohun Roy.*

② *The French* Tricolore.

③ *The sun flag of the Indian National Society, 1883.*

④ *The lotus, an ancient Indian symbol, depicted on an India postage stamp.*

⑤ *Sister Nivedita.*

⑥

Durga. According to legend, *vajra* was created from the bones of Rishi Dadhichi. It is a symbol of supreme sacrifice.

In 1905, the British rulers under Lord Curzon initiated the Partition of Bengal which was a major turning point in the Indian independence movement. Sister Nivedita played a pioneering role in organising the anti-Partition movement in Bengal.

Sister Nivedita's flag, prepared by the students of her girls' school in Calcutta, was displayed for public viewing at the Congress exhibition in December 1906. The flag was square in shape and adorned by the symbol of the *vajra* placed in between the words *'Bande'* and *'Mataram'* written in Bengali with 108 *jyotis* or flames embroidered along the outer periphery. *Bande Mataram*, which is also spelled as *Vande Mataram* means 'Hail to the Mother'. The number 108 is considered to be most auspicious for both Hindus and Buddhists. The traditional *japa malas* or prayer beads have 108 beads that are used to count the repetitions of prayers, chants or devotions. The number is a perfect three-digit multiple of three, its components adding up to nine, which is three threes. Three represents supreme balance.

⑦

Sister Nivedita's flag is preserved in the Acharya Bhavan Museum, the erstwhile residence of Acharya Jagadish Chandra Bose in Kolkata. Using 'R.S.' as nom de plume, Sister Nivedita strongly advocated the *vajra* as the national flag for India in an article titled 'The *Vajra* as a National Flag' which was published in the *Modern Review* in November 1909 (perhaps, this was the first printed article on the subject in India). She wrote in the opening sentences of the article that,

> The question of the invention of a flag for India is beginning to be discussed in the press. Those who contemplate the desirability of such a symbol, seem to be unaware that already a great many people have taken up, and are using, the ancient Indian Vajra or Thunderbolt, in this way. When we look at all that a national banner means...[5]

Sister Nivedita died in 1911 in Darjeeling; her epitaph aptly reads, 'Here reposes Sister Nivedita who gave her all to India.'

The first *Swadeshi* flag inscribed with the slogan *Bande Mataram* was created in 1905–1906, during the period that Rajani Palme Dutt (1896–1974), an acclaimed journalist and theoretician in the Communist Party of Great Britain, termed as the first great wave of national struggle. The flag was defiantly unfurled on 7 August 1906 at Greer Park, opposite University Science College at Upper Circular Road in Calcutta. The day was being observed as Boycott Day, the first anniversary of Lord Curzon's proclamation of the Partition of Bengal. No sooner than the Partition of Bengal was declared, thousands of volunteers protested the decision in a unanimous voice chanting the newly-discovered war cry *Bande Mataram*. The song soon spread beyond the boundaries of the state of Bengal and throughout India and would eventually reunite Bengal in 1911, the same year India's capital was shifted from Calcutta to Delhi.

Several *Swadeshi* postcards were in use during the anti-partition movement (1905–1911) in Bengal and in other parts of India. The *Swadeshi* postcards were in great demand in

⑧

⑥ *Maharshi Dadhichi.*

⑦ *Sister Nivedita's flag.*

⑧ *The first* Swadeshi *flag or* Bande Mataram *flag or Calcutta flag, 1906.*

⑨ *Patriotic postcard of 1905; the cachet shows a portrait of Surendra Nath Banerjea.*

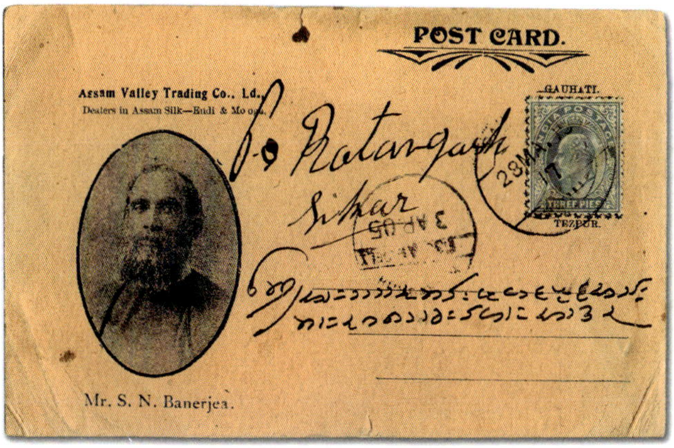

⑨

response to the historic call of 'Boycott British Goods'. Surendra Nath Banerjea who was at the forefront of the nationalist movements was featured in many such patriotic national stationery items.

The Calcutta flag was designed jointly by Sachindra Prasad Basu, Secretary of the Anti-Circular Society[6] and Sukumar Mitra, a close associate of Surendra Nath Banerjea. Dr Bhupendranath Dutta (younger brother of Swami Vivekananda), revolutionary and editor of the Bengali daily *Jugantar*, commented in his book *Bharater Dwitiya Swadhinater Sangram—Aprakashita Rajnaitik Itihas* (India's Second War of Independence—The Untold Political History, 1926), that Sachindra Prasad Basu and Sukumar Mitra were inspired by the French *Tricolore* and its message of *Liberte, Egalite* and *Fraternite*. The flag was approved by, amongst others, Asutosh Chowdhury and Abdul Halim Gajhnavi in a meeting called by Surendra Nath Banerjea at the Indian Association Hall in Calcutta. The flag was hoisted on 7 August 1906. The day was being observed as 'Boycott Day', the first anniversary of the Partition of Bengal. On this day Narendranath Sen, who was then the editor of the *Indian Mirror*, consecrated the new flag. Bhupendra Nath Basu (who later became the president of the Madras session of the Congress in 1914) carried the flag to Surendra Nath Banerjea, who in turn hoisted it for the first time.

10

11

The *Bande Mataram* flag was again hoisted by the Congress President Dadabhai Naoroji, the Grand Old Man of India at the Calcutta session of the Congress in December 1906.

The song *'Bande Mataram'* was composed in 1876 by Bankim Chandra Chatterjee. In 1882 the song was incorporated in his novel *Ananda Math* (Abode of Bliss). It was set to music by Rabindranath

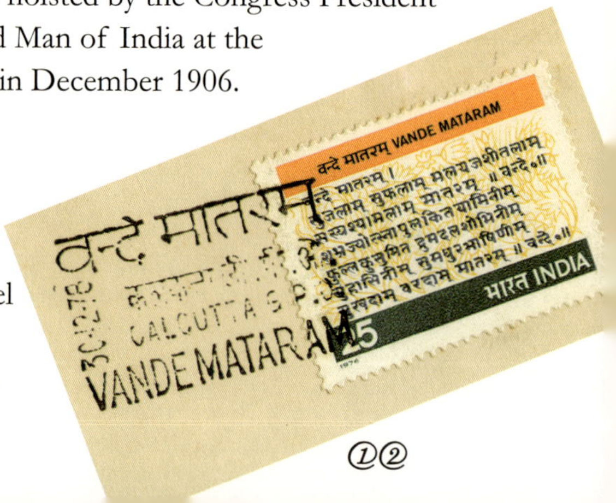

12

Tagore who also sang it for the first time at the Calcutta Congress session in 1896. During the turbulent days of the anti-Partition movement in Bengal, its appeal was instant. The slogan *'Bande Mataram'* became the war cry of national resurgence. The amazing transformation of *Bande Mataram* from an innocent song into a revolutionary slogan was the work of the youth in Bengal in 1905–1906. Bipin Chandra Pal and Sri Aurobindo adopted *Bande Mataram* as the name of their English daily in 1906 that was to serve as the organ of revolutionary nationalism from Calcutta. In 1908, the *Bande Mataram* was forced to stop publication under the Newspapers Act of 1908. Madame Cama with Har Dayal as editor started afresh another revolutionary journal by the same name from Geneva in September 1909. They launched the journal with the object of continuing the good work perpetuated by the original *Bande Mataram* founded by Bipin Chandra Pal.

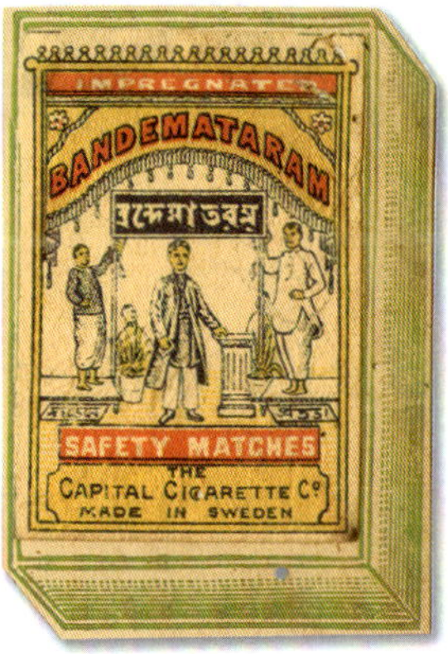

13

10 *Surendra Nath Banerjea.*

11 *Dadabhai Naoroji*

12 *'Vande Mataram' song in Hindi on a stamp depicting colours of the* Swadeshi *flag.*

13 *A matchbox with the 'Bande Mataram' slogan printed on its cover in English and Bengali.*

Parallelism in History

A strikingly similar flag to the Calcutta one, with minor deviations, was waved by Bhikaiji Rustom Cama on 22 August 1907 at the Second International Socialist Congress in Stuttgart, Germany. Waving the flag Madame Cama declared,

> This flag is of Indian independence. Behold it is born. It is already sanctioned by the blood of martyred Indian youths. I call upon you, gentlemen, to rise and salute this flag of Indian Independence. In the name of this flag, I appeal to lovers of freedom all over the world to cooperate with this flag in freeing one-fifth of the human race.[7]

The *Leipziger Zeitung* mentioned the appearance of exotic Mrs Kramas (Madame Cama) from India, dressed in shimmering silken garments, as the undoubted culmination of the International Socialist Congress. She assumed the rostrum and appealed to the Congress to help the people oppressed by England and at last displayed a silken tricolour—the banner of the oppressed. Then the cheers of the international crowd would not end.

Dr Bhupendranath Dutta, who researched in great details about the genesis of the *Bande Mataram* flag in his book *Bharater Dwitiya Swadhinater Sangram—Aprakashita Rajnaitik Itihas*, tells us that it was Hemchandra Kanungo (Das) who made the flag for Madame Cama, when he was in Paris. Dr Dutta further mentions that Khasi Rao, the revolutionary brother of Madhav Rao, a general in the army of the Baroda state, had gone to Switzerland to undergo military training. He had carried with him a small replica of the Calcutta flag given to him by the Bengal Congress leaders. In Geneva, Khasi Rao met Hemchandra Kanungo. Madame Cama wrote in a leaflet titled 'Bande Mataram – A Message to the People of India' (1908), 'This flag of

Bande Mataram, which I wave before you, was made for me by a noble selfless young patriot [Hemchandra Kanungo], who is now standing at the bar of the so-called court of justice in our country. What a mockery to talk of justice and jury!'[8]

17

16

On 19 December 1908, Madame Cama attended one of a series of lectures on 'Indian Nationalism' delivered by Bipin Chandra Pal in London. At the end of his speech, Madame Cama demanded a hearing waving the tricolour flag. In her speech she said, 'This is the flag for which Khudiram and Prafulla Chaki died.'[9]

18

After World War I she had to remain in exile and was allowed to return to India only when her health deteriorated in 1935. Madame Cama quietly passed away in Bombay (Mumbai) on 16 August 1936, unsung and unmourned. The undaunted lady wrote for her tombstone in French and Gujarati, 'Resistance to tyranny is obedience to God'—her most befitting epitaph. She had left behind her original flag with Madhav Rao in Paris, who in turn passed it on to Indulal Kanaiyalal Yagnik, a socialist leader from Gujarat.

Indulal Yagnik (1892–1972) clandestinely brought the flag along with other records into India and kept it at a secret location in Bombay. In 1937, when Yagnik was interned in Yervada jail in Poona (Pune), he got the opportunity to meet G.V. Ketkar, grandson of Bal Gangadhar Tilak and former editor of the *Kesari* and *Tarun Bharat*. Yagnik told him how he had smuggled the flag unfurled by Madame Cama into India and also about its present whereabouts. Ketkar retrieved the original flag from the secret place.

14 Madame Cama.

15 Portrait of Madame Cama with the flag that she famously waved at the Second International Socialist Congress in Stuttgart, Germany in 1907.

16 Prafulla Chaki.

17 Khudiram Bose.

18 Indulal Yagnik.

Veer Savarkar on 26 October 1937 publicly unveiled the flag in Poona with much fanfare. The framed flag is preserved for public viewing in the Tilak Museum of Maratha and Kesari Library in Pune.

India's first female prime minister, Mrs Indira Gandhi, paid her tribute in her 'Foreword' to the book *Madame Cama – Mother of Indian Revolution* by Dr Panchanan Saha: 'We remember specially her bold action and pioneering work to popularise our national flag. It is the tricolour she unfurled which was adopted with some alternation by our freedom movement.'[10]

Home Rule Flag, 1917

At the time of the Home Rule movement in 1917, Dr Annie Besant and B.P. Wadia, in consultation with Bal Gangadhar Tilak and Mohammad Ali Jinnah, devised the Home Rule flag.

19

20

The Home Rule flag had five red stripes representing Hindus and four green stripes for Muslims placed in between the red stripes, superimposed with seven stars representing the *Saptarishi* configuration (Great Bear constellation) typical of the seven wise sages of India, said to be the founders of Indian civilisation. The rishis (sages) are Bhrigu, Atri, Angirasa, Vasishta, Pulastya, Pulaha and Kratu. According to legend, the stars representing the rishis bring down to earth the required knowledge and energies to strengthen the processes of transition. The flag also had the symbols of a crescent moon and a star of the Muslims. On the canton there was the British Union Jack. The inclusion of the Union Jack, symbolising the goal of dominion status that the movement sought to achieve, however, was not met with a favourable

22

21

response. The Home Rule flag was hoisted at the Calcutta session of the Congress in 1917 under the presidentship of Dr Besant. The flag, however, failed to generate enough support and fell into oblivion shortly.

19 *This stamp released on 1 October 1963 is wrongly dated as 1837–1933. Dr Besant was born in 1847 not 1837.*

20 *The all-Hindi 'Tilak Janambhumi' birthplace cancellation applied on the FDC from Ratnagiri, the birthplace of Lokmanya Keshav 'Bal' Tilak, to commemorate his birth centenary on 23 July 1956.*

21 *The Home Rule flag.*

22 *Mohammad Ali Jinnah.*

Endnotes:

1. Suniti Kumar Chatterji, *The National Flag* (Calcutta: Mitra & Ghosh, 1944); vide Appendix III.
2. Sophia Dobson Collet, ed. and compiled, *The Life and Letters of Raja Rammohan Roy* (Calcutta: A.C. Sarkar, 1914), p. 178.
3. *The Modern Review*, October 1930, p. 482.
4. Bhagavad Gita (5:10).
5. The full text is provided in Appendix I.
6. The Anti-Circular Society was formed in 1905 under the patronage of the Dawn Society of Calcutta to protest against a secret circular of the British government disbanding students taking part in politics.
7. Khorshed Adi Sethna, *Madame Bhikaiji Rustom Cama* (New Delhi: Publications Division, 1987), pp. 1–2.
8. Ibid., p. 67.
9. Lt. Cdr. K.V. Singh, *Our National Flag* (New Delhi: Publications Division, 1991), p. 31.
10. Indira Gandhi, Foreword in *Madame Cama–Mother of Indian Revolution* by Dr Panchanan Saha (Calcutta: Manisha Granthalay, 1975).

Birth of the Swaraj Flag

The *Swadeshi* flag-hoisting ceremony by Sir Dadabhai Naoroji at the 22nd session of the Congress in Calcutta in 1906, evoked huge euphoria that left a permanent impact on Pingali Venkayya's mind, who was a delegate at the Congress session. Intrigued by the national flag, Pingali Venkayya (1876–1963), hailing from Masulipatam (Machilipatnam), founded the Indian National Flag Mission and relentlessly pursued his goal to give shape to a distinctive national flag to be accepted by all. In 1916 Venkayya came up with a booklet titled 'A National Flag for India' in which he put forth about twenty-four designs for the Indian flag. Mahatma Gandhi in an article titled 'The National Flag' published in the *Young India* in April 1921 acknowledged,

> Whilst I have always admired the persistent zeal in which Mr Venkayya has prosecuted the cause of a National Flag at every session of the Congress for the past four years, he has never able (sic) to enthuse me; and in his designs I saw nothing to stir the nation to its depths ...[1]

①

Sister Nivedita's *Vajra* flag had also found place among the flag designs made by Venkayya in his booklet after undertaking research into various flags from across the world. A noticeable feature of Venkayya's flags was the presence of a small Union Jack in most of his designs.

In April 1921, prior to the Bezwada (now, Vijayawada) Congress, Mahatma Gandhi asked Venkayya to prepare a design which should contain a *charkha* (spinning

(2)

wheel) on a red (Hindu colour) and green (Muslim colour) background. The *charkha* was placed on the flag apropos of the suggestion made by Lala Hansraj of Jullundur (Jalandhar). Later, on maturer consideration of Mahatma Gandhi, a white band, representing the other religions, was added on top of the colour green. Gandhi explained in his article 'The National Flag',

(3)

> The white portion is intended to represent all other faiths. The weakest numerically occupy the first place. The Islamic colour comes next; the Hindu colour red comes last, the idea being that the strongest should act as a shield to the weakest ... to represent the equality of the least of us with the best, an equal part is suggested to all three colours in the design. ...The regulation size of the flag should contain the drawing of a full sized spinning-wheel.

Thus the first *Swaraj* flag (flag of self-government) with a *charkha* on a 'white over green over red' background was born.

(1) *Some of the flag designs made by Venkayya (from the booklet 'A National Flag for India').*

(2) *FDC featuring Pingali Venkayya alongside his flags.*

(3) *Postmark commemorating Venkayya's birth centenary celebrations.*

④

The *Swaraj* flag was never officially adopted as the 'national flag' by a formal resolution by the INC. Nevertheless, Mahatma Gandhi's approval made the *Swaraj* flag acceptable to the people in general.

Many labels issued defying the government orders were affixed on postal articles for the *Swadeshi* propaganda (see illustration 4). Repeated postal notices were issued from time to time prohibiting the use of such labels on postal articles. Postal articles found affixed with such labels were sent to the Dead Letter Office (DLO) for disposal.

Nagpur Flag Satyagraha, 1923

The incidents which took place initially in Jabalpur and then spread to Nagpur and other places in central India with regard to flag processions in 1923, clearly showed how the common people had become awakened to the necessity of possessing a national symbol such as a flag. The ban imposed in Nagpur on the display of the *Swaraj* flag had produced counter results. The flag, which was not even adopted by a formal resolution, proved significantly its efficacy as the symbol of national aspiration and pride as it became the rallying point of a common sentiment.

Subhadra Kumari Chauhan was the first person to court arrest for hoisting the *Swaraj* flag at Jabalpur on 18 March 1923. C. Rajagopalachari wrote:

> No Indian can fail to see the intensity of feeling and courage which must lead an Indian sister to give herself up to the custody of the class from which police constables came and head constable came. No greater calamity could be

⑤

imagined for a Hindu or a Musalman lady; but the wonderful revolution we are in has changed all this, and for the revolution of our right to live and move erect on the land of our birth, this frail sister of tender years has shown the way to us all. [2]

⑥

Subhadra Kumari, on being released from Jabalpur, joined the Nagpur Satyagraha and was arrested again on 11 May 1923 for carrying the flag through a prohibited area.

⑦

Vinoba Bhave was one of the moving spirits behind the Nagpur flag Satyagraha.

Seth Jamnalal Bajaj had taken the lead organisational role in the Nagpur flag Satyagraha which started on 13 April, the anniversary of the Jallianwala Bagh tragedy. Jamnalal was arrested on 17 June and the very next day, that is, 18 June 1923, was declared to be 'All India Flag Day' as a mark of protest.

Makhan Lal Chaturvedi led the procession on 18 June 1923 observed as the 'All India Flag Day'. The flag Satyagraha no longer remained a local issue; volunteers from different parts of India poured into Nagpur to join the agitation.

On 22 July, Sardar Vallabhbhai Patel arrived at Nagpur to join the flag Satyagraha.

⑧

⑨

④ *Stamp-like Cinderella labels, displaying the* Swaraj *flag, conveying exhortations to 'Boycott British Goods' and/or depicting portraits of leaders of the Civil Disobedience movement containing the words* 'Swatantra Bharat'.

⑤ *Subhadra Kumari Chauhan.*

⑥ *Vinoba Bhave.*

⑦ *Seth Jamnalal Bajaj.*

⑧ *Makhan Lal Chaturvedi.*

⑨ *Sardar Vallabhbhai Patel.*

On 17 August he brought the flag Satyagraha to an honourable end.

①@

Sardar Vithalbhai Patel arranged the release order for all the volunteers arrested in connection with the flag Satyagraha in Nagpur.

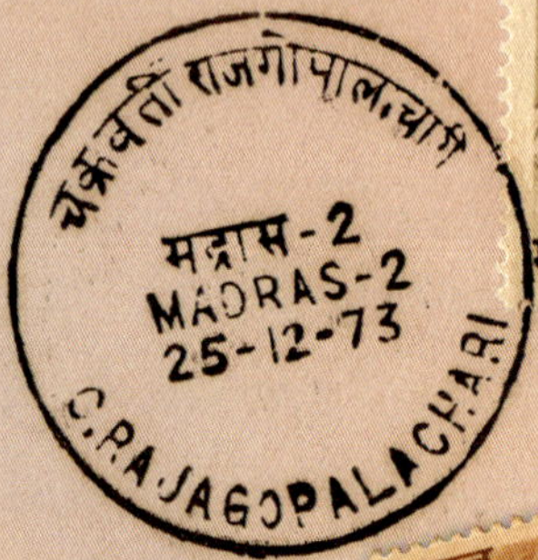

A series of articles by C. Rajagopalachari was published in *Young India* in support of the Nagpur flag Satyagraha and subsequently compiled in a booklet titled 'India's Flag':

①①

> You don't find on our flag a tiger or a lion or a unicorn but a charkha. It represents industry, goodwill and our new weapon against brute force. The government wouldn't have minded if we had put the sign of a gun on it, as they have bigger guns. But the *charkha*, represents 300 million *charkhas* and the British could not resist its force.[3]

①②

He went on to elaborate as reported in *The Hindu* on 8 June 1923,

> The secret is that the Government do not like the combination of the three colours in this flag. If an individual Christian or Persi carried a white flag, a Hindu a red flag, or a Musalman a green flag, the government would not have interfered. All the colours put together in a flag presented a danger to the British Empire.

Black Flag Demonstration

In 1927, the British Government set up a commission of seven members of the British Parliament, headed by Sir John Simon to study the workings of the government in India and to recommend further reforms to be executed. The Simon Commission did not include a single Indian. The Congress took offence at the omission. When the members of the commission arrived in India in February 1928, people expressed their feelings of protest against the unwanted commission wherever they went.

The demonstrators marched in processions waving black flags and carrying banners with the slogan 'SIMON GO BACK'.

①③

Punjab *Kesari* (the lion of Punjab) Lala Lajpat Rai (1865–1928) was severely beaten up by the police in one such demonstration against the Simon Commission in Lahore (now in Pakistan) and succumbed to his injuries. In 1928 Bhagat Singh (1907–1931) and his group formed the Hindustan Socialist Republican Association (HSRA). The HSRA decided to avenge the death of Lala Lajpat Rai. On 8 April 1929, Bhagat Singh and Batukeshwar Dutta threw bombs in the Central Legislative Assembly in an attempt to threaten the government. They were arrested immediately. Bhagat Singh was hanged to death on 23 March 1931 charged with murder. Shaheed Bhagat Singh's martyrdom prompted youths in India to join en masse to fight for India's independence.

①④

Harkishen Singh Surjeet was sentenced to one year's rigorous imprisonment in 1932 for bringing down the British flag and hoisting the *Swaraj* flag in its place, on the first anniversary of Bhagat Singh's martyrdom at the district court at Hoshiarpur in Jalandhar. People fondly named him *Surjeet aka London Tod Singh* or 'One who breaks London'.

On 29 December 1929 the Congress met at Lahore for the 44th session. At midnight on New Year's Eve, the Congress President Jawaharlal Nehru hoisted the *Swaraj* flag upon the banks of the river Ravi in Lahore. The flag was perched atop a 115-feet tall flagstaff, hoisted by a mechanical device. Since the event took place at midnight, the top of the flag-mast was

①⓪ *C. Rajagopalachari.*

①① *Sardar Vithalbhai Patel.*

①② *'India's Flag' by C. Rajagopalachari.*

①③ *Lala Lajpat Rai.*

①④ *Bhagat Singh.*

illuminated with powerful electric lights. A 'pledge of Independence' was read out. Nehru declared *Purna Swaraj* (complete independence) as the goal and gave a nationwide call to observe 26 January of 1930 as Independence Day.

The flag on a Cinderella label issued from Khadi Mondal, Calcutta (see illustration 15), has the words 'Observe 26 January as Independence Day'. It has a stanza from *Padmini Upakhyan* (The Saga of Padmini, 1858) originally penned by the nineteenth-century Bengali poet Rangalal Bandopadhyay:

15

Swadhitanata hinatay ke bachite chay?
Dashatya srinkhal bolo ke dharibay pa-ey?

(Who wishes to live without freedom?
Who wishes to be fettered by slavery?)

The *Swaraj* flag and Civil Disobedience movements

The years following the flag Satyagraha in 1923 were crucial in the history of the Indian freedom struggle. Many historic events took place where the *Swaraj* flag was pivotal. On 12 March 1930 Mahatma Gandhi launched Salt Satyagraha and set out from Sabarmati ashram with his volunteers to Dandi on the Gujarat coast. The twenty-five-day long march culminated on 6 April 1930. It was a campaign for the non-violent movement against the British salt monopoly in India, which eventually grew into the Civil Disobedience movement and drew more volunteers to join the freedom struggles.

The miniature sheet issued to commemorate the 75th anniversary of Salt Satyagraha by India Post in 2005 (see illustration 16), captures the historic moment and the varied facets of Salt Satyagraha. The fluttering *Swaraj* flag is depicted on the top margin of the miniature sheet, while the first stamp (clockwise) catches a glimpse of the marchers, led by Mahatma Gandhi, on the move. The second stamp shows Mahatma Gandhi while the headlines in the *Bombay Chronicle*, dated 13 March 1930, announces the beginning of the 'Great March for Liberty'. The third stamp displays lines written by Gandhi on 5 April 1930, 'I want world sympathy in this battle of right against might.' The fourth stamp depicts Gandhi picking up a lump of salt and the course traversed during the Dandi March.

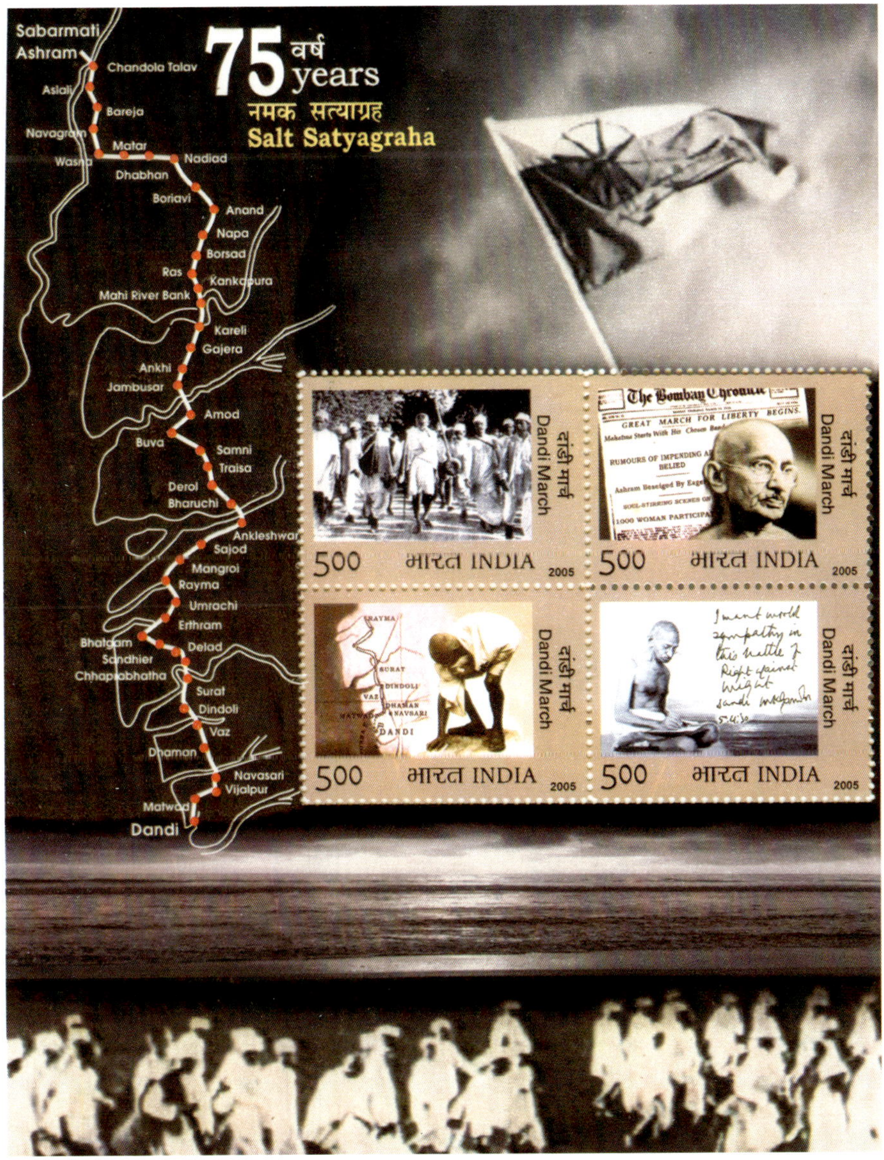

16

The *Swaraj* flag was also hoisted in Japan around this time. Reuters reported, quoting Tokyo newspapers, that on 12 March 1930, the Indian nationalists in Japan including Rashbehari Bose celebrated the beginning of Gandhi's campaign by gathering at Kamakura and hoisting the Congress flag which they vowed to keep flying till victory was achieved. The site was said to be that selected by Dr Sun Yat Sen for similar demonstrations before starting the Nationalist Revolution in China.

15 Swaraj *flag on a Cinderella label.*

16 *Miniature sheet (issued in 2005) commemorating the 75th anniversary of Salt Satyagraha.*

17

18

19

During the Civil Disobedience movement of 1930, Bishwanath Roy, then a student of law, and his two associates, were fired upon by the police while hoisting the *Swaraj* flag at Ghantaghar in Allahabad. This resulted in the killing of his associates. Bishwanath Roy was arrested and imprisoned for the act.

②⓪

②①

Surjya Sen (1894–1934) affectionately called 'Master-da', set up an effective revolutionary organisation—the Chittagong Republican Army (CRA). On 18 April 1930, CRA seized power in Chittagong (now in Bangladesh) through a sudden attack and British rule ceased to exist for a while. He was captured in 1933 and hanged on 12 January 1934.

①⑦ *Rashbehari Bose.*

①⑧ *During the Civil Disobedience movements of 1930–1931, there were several 'flag processions' organised by the Congress volunteers throughout India. They waved* Swaraj *flags and festoons inscribed with slogans such as: 'Up, up with the National Flag. Down, down with the Union Jack.'*

①⑨ *Bishwanath Roy.*

②⓪ *Surjya Sen: stamp issued by India.*

②① *Surjya Sen: stamp and postmark issued by Bangladesh.*

Endnotes:

1. Vide Appendix II.
2. C. Rajagopalachari, '*India's Flag*' (Madras: Ganesh & Co., 1923).
3. Arundhati Virmani, 'National Symbols under Colonial Domination: The Nationalization of the Indian Flag, March-August 1923', *Past and Present*, 164 (1999), p. 180.

Conflicts around the Swaraj Flag

The projection of the Congress flag, alias the *Swaraj* flag, as the national flag for the Indian federation as a whole was not taken kindly by the Convention and the Feudatory States, collectively described as Princely States of the British Empire in India, as well as by certain other political parties both at the regional and national levels. The *Swaraj* flag for the whole of India was considered to be a threat to their identity and authority. In fact, many Princely States stuck to their distinctive insignia as the symbols of their territorial autonomy. A few Princely States continued to fly their banners even after India's Independence in 1947. However, with the abolition of Privy Purses in 1971, all the erstwhile Princely States had to give up their respective flags.

On the other hand, in the 1920s, when the political atmosphere was surcharged with the spirit of the Khilafat movement and communal compartmentalism, Prof. S.K. Chatterji in *The National Flag* wrote, 'the communal interpretation of the colours of the "Swaraj flag" came into being—Green was made to represent the Muhammadans, Red the Hindus, and the neutral White—all other lesser communities.' The *Swaraj* flag, meant to create harmony, became a symbol of dispute and eventually failed to find a pan-Indian acceptance.

The Khilafat movement (1919–1924) was a Muslim religious movement aimed at, and united against, the British government in India apparently to support restoration of the Ottoman (Turkish) empire ruled by the *Khalifa*, considered to be the custodian of Islam. The Khilafat leaders had assured full support to the Congress in their fight for freedom. It was termed a national movement when the Congress and the Khilafat leaders promised to work and fight together for the causes of Khilafat and *Swaraj*. However, when Turkey became a Republic in 1923, the Khilafat movement lost its relevance and the movement was phased out in 1924.

②

Maulana Mohammad Ali Jauhar, leader of the Khilafat movement, had earlier served the Muslim League as its President in 1918. Later he joined the Congress party and became its President at the 38th session of the Congress held in Cocanada (present day Kakinada) from 23 December 1923 to 1 January 1924. Thus he holds a rare distinction of heading two major political parties which were at loggerheads with each other. At the flag hoisting ceremony of the Congress, Md. Ali Jauhar urged the countrymen to forget their differences and stop thinking of themselves as Hindus and Muslims,

③

> For you are all of one faith in defence of the National flag ... as commanded by you, I am here to unfurl the flag of the nation. This flag is nothing if it is not the flag of Freedom. But it cannot be (sic) flag of Freedom unless it is also the flag of our national unity.[1]

Md Ali Jauhar left the All India Congress in 1928.

The All India Muslim League used the Islamic *'Subz Hilali Parcham'* meaning 'green flag with the crescent', since its inception in 1906, in Dacca (Dhaka)—present-day capital of the People's Republic of Bangladesh. After the breakdown of Congress–Khilafat alliance in 1924, the Muslim League's attitude also changed. They were no longer inclined to accept the *Swaraj* flag as the sole symbol of India's nationhood. At the All India Muslim League's Lucknow session in 1940,

Mohammad Ali Jinnah pronounced the Islamic green flag to be the national flag for the 'Land of the Pure'. The 'Pakistan Resolution' was adopted in Lahore on 23 March 1940. Begum Hafeezuddin, leader of the women volunteers of the All India Muslim League, called upon the Muslims of the subcontinent to unite under the *Subz Hilali Parcham*. It was on 4 August 1947 that Pakistan's national flag was created by adding a narrow white stripe at the hoist side to represent the minority communities and also to enable the national flag to be distinguished from that of the Muslim League's flag. Ameer-ud-din Khidwai is credited as the designer of the Pakistani national flag.

The Statesman on 8 August 1947 carried a news under the heading 'Mr. Gandhi to Spend Rest of his life in Pakistan' wherein it was reported that in reply to a question by Dr Lehna Singh, General Secretary, Punjab

Provincial Congress Committee, Mr Gandhi said that if the Pakistan flag was such as would ensure equal rights and full protection to the minorities, they should all accept and honour the flag and have absolutely no hesitation in saluting it. *The Statesman* quoted Gandhi saying: 'I would ask you not to disown the Pakistan flag merely because it bears a crescent.' He added: 'I must, however, say that, if no assurance of the kind I have mentioned is forthcoming, at least I shall refuse to salute that flag.'

⑤

Sikh opposition to the *Swaraj* colours also gained momentum around the same time, and possibly as early as in 1921. In 1929, a deputation of the Sikhs met Mahatma Gandhi at Lahore and made a definite demand that the Sikh colour, a shade of yellow or black, be added to the *Swaraj* flag. In March 1930, when Gandhi launched the Civil Disobedience movement, Baba Kharak Singh, the president of the Shiromani Gurdwara Prabandhak Committee, reportedly refused to join the Movement unless and until the Sikh colour was incorporated into the flag.

⑥

In 1924, the All India Sanskrit Conference, which met at Sanskrit College, Calcutta, suggested inclusion of the saffron or ochre colour and a *gada* (mace) of Lord Vishnu in the national flag.

On the eve of the Bezwada session of the Congress in 1924, Rev. C.F. Andrews, Dwijendranath Tagore, Vidhusekhar Bhattacharya, Kalidas Nag, Bhimrao Sastri, J.J. Vakil, Premsundar Basu, Marichi (Hirjibhai P. Morriswala), Nepalchandra Ray and N. Aiyaswami jointly sent a letter addressed to Gandhi suggesting the inclusion of the *gairika (geru)* or ochre colour in the flag.

①, ②, ③ Maulana Mohammad Ali Jauhar.

④ Inland letter sheet commemorating the golden jubilee of the 'Pakistan Resolution'.

⑤ Baba Kharak Singh.

⑥ Sanskrit College, Calcutta.

It was claimed by D.V. Sivarao, the learned research scholar of Andhra Pradesh, in a broadcast from All India Radio in Vijaywada on 10 October 1953, that the idea of the substitution of the *chakra* (wheel) for the *charkha* (spinning wheel) was first conceived in May 1925, by 'Andhra Ratna' (Jewel of Andhra) D. Gopalakrishnayya (better known as Hero of Chirala-Perala). To Gopalakrishnayya, Mahatma Gandhi's *charkha* flag was a mere spinners–weavers' flag.

> If the flag were to symbolize the Nation's soul and its Sadhana, both Bhakti and Mukti must be indicated, and with plenty of graceful and incessant movement… A simple 'Charka' may exhibit the sorrow of the stomach merely. It is puerile to think that it suffices to indicate the Nation's condition and concern.[2]

Gopalakrishnayya devised as early as in 1920 two flags for his *Goshti* and *Rama Dandu*. The main component of their symbolism was a *Vajra*, or a wheel made out of the bone of Maharshi Dadhichi.

Rabindranath Tagore was at variance with Mahatma Gandhi's advocacy of the *charkha* symbol. In 1924–1925, a debate ensued between Tagore and Gandhi on the *charkha* campaign. In an essay titled *'Swaraj Sadhan'* (Attaining Freedom) Tagore argued the futility of the spinning of the *charkha* as a means to attain *Swaraj* (self-government).

The Flag Committee, 1931

The Congress Working Committee (CWC), which met at Karachi on 2 April 1931, passed a resolution stressing the need for a flag which would be acceptable to all. In pursuance of the resolution, a seven-member Flag Committee was formed with Dr Pattabhi Sitaramayya, as the Convener, to go into the question of the national flag for recommending a new flag after examining the objections raised against the present *Swaraj* flag.

⑧

⑨

⑩

⑪

Jawaharlal Nehru, Abul Kalam Azad, Sardar Vallabhbhai Patel, Master Tara Singh, Dr N.S. Hardikar and Kaka Saheb Kalelkar were the other members of the Flag Committee of 1931.

Dr Pattabhi Sitaramayya, in his capacity as the Convener of the Flag Committee, issued a three-point questionnaire dated 23 April 1931 to all Provincial Congress Committees, eminent personalities, and well-known social organisations, inviting their opinions on the choice in regard to the design of the national flag.

⑫

⑦ FDC released on the occasion of the birth centenary of Rabindranath Tagore on 7 May 1961. The FDC issued from Santiniketan is autographed by Satyajit Ray, the designer of the stamp and an alumnus of Visva-Bharati University.

⑧ Kakasaheb Kalelkar.

⑨ Master Tara Singh.

⑩ Abul Kalam Azad.

⑪ Sardar Vallabhbhai Patel.

⑫ Dr Pattabhi Sitaramayya.

Masulipatnam
23.4.1931

Dear Sir,

Permit me to bring to your notice that the following resolution regarding the National Flag was passed by the Working Committee at its meeting held on April 2, 1931.

Text of the resolution:

"Whereas the National Flag now in vogue has gained in popularity by usage and convention and whereas objection has been taken to the three colours in the Flag on the ground that, they are conceived on a communal basis, the Working Committee hereby appoints a Committee for the purpose of examining the objections and recommending a flag for the acceptance of the Congress. The Committee shall have the authority to take such evidence as it may consider necessary and to send its report and recommendations to the Working Committee on or before July 31, 1931."

May I request you to answer the following questions in particular, and send up your suggestions in the matter.

1. Is there any feeling amongst any group of people or community in your province, in regard to the design of the National Flag, which in your opinion should be taken into consideration by this Committee?
2. Have you any specific suggestions for making the Flag more popular?
3. Is there any defect or drawback in the design now in vogue, which, you consider, demands attention?

Note: Let me submit that in sending up your suggestions, you will be greatly adding to their weight if you take the trouble of accompanying them with a flag preferably in cloth so as to illustrate your ideas.

Further, I would suggest that these replies might be sent up by the PCCs and the public by the end of May. If the Committee considers it necessary, it will ask you to tender oral evidence later.

Yours sincerely,
B. Pattabhi Sitaramayya
Convener, Flag Committee[3]

Earlier Jawaharlal Nehru in his letter to Pattabhi Sitaramayya, dated 12 April 1931, amply clarified his ideas on the flag question:

Mr. Dear Pattabhi,

I have your letter, I agree with you that the questionnaire suggested by you should be sent to the Provincial Congress Committees and to the Press. I am very much interested in the flag question, but I may be away for the next few weeks, I am, therefore, giving you below some very rough ideas of mine on the subject.

1. Ordinarily, I would be greatly averse to changing the present flag, which has become very popular, but having regard to the circumstances, perhaps some change is necessary. This change, however, should not interfere too much with the present flag.
2. We should make it perfectly clear that our flag is not based on communal considerations. Perhaps some change is necessary. This change, however, should not interfere too much with the present flag.
3. The present arrangement with white at the top is bad, as the white does not show unless there is a colour background. Therefore, in any event the white should either be put in the centre or should give place to another colour.
4. The present flag is I believe, identical with the Bulgarian flag. This is undesirable.
5. I am inclined to think that the colour white should give place to a basanti colour or light saffron. My reason for this is not that the Sikhs desire it as their colour, but because this colour is an old Indian colour and is associated with sacrifice in our past history. Further, this colour has been adopted by the women of India and it would be graceful and deserving tribute to the women to order this colour. The exact shade of the colour should be carefully considered. The place of the colour in the flag must also be considered from the aesthetic point of view. Thus, it may be either at the top or at the centre.
6. I should like to retain both red and green as they are beautiful colours.
7. The final design chosen should be that which satisfies the aesthetic sense and should be in accordance with the heraldic principles.

These are some suggestions made on the spur of the moment just to give you some idea of what I have got in my mind.

Yours sincerely,

J.N.[4]

13

The Flag Committee received several suggestions. There were many suggestive 'letters to the editor' published in national dailies with regard to the flag question.

Professor S.K. Chatterji, after consulting some of the best intellects of the country, such as Dr Kalidas Nag amongst others, presented before the Flag Committee and the public, some suggestions for what they are worth through an article titled 'The National Flag' published in the *Modern Review* in June 1931. He cautioned in that article that any explanation of the colours of our national flag as symbolic of Hindus, Musalmans, Christians and any other communities, should be regarded as pernicious and anti-national. He reiterated that a communal explanation or allocation of colours, like communal electorates, should be considered taboo.

14

15

16

17

18

Professor Chatterji further pointed out that red, white and green are three colours whose combination has already figured in the flags of at least four different countries: Persia, Italy, Bulgaria and Mexico. The dispositions of the colours are different, but Bulgaria has an identical arrangement with the present Indian flag. He wondered why India could not have something distinctive. In order to avoid chances of confusing our national flag with that of other nations, Professor Chatterji suggested vertical bands of red, green and ochre or saffron, with the three or four-spoked wheel (or the four or eight-petalled white lotus) in the central field. Then the flag may be described as *'Hindustan-ka Tiranga'* (flag of Hindustan) or *'Chauranga Jhanda'* (flag of four colours). The cloth for the national flag should in all cases be hand-spun and hand-woven, whether it be cotton or silk.[5]

19

T. Ramaswami Chowdary, the '*Kaviraju*' (as he is known in Andhra Pradesh), based on his understanding and critical study and analysis of the Vedas, Upanishads and Puranas, sent a design of a flag to the Flag Committee named *'Pranava-Pataka'*. It had an outer ring of black, a central ring of red and an inner spot of white, representing the qualities of *tamas*, *rajas* and *sattva* (dullness, passion and goodness) respectively.

Pandit Madan Mohan Malaviya advocated for an all-saffron flag to represent the united Indian nation and not simply a community in particular, whether it be Hindus, Muslims or Sikhs. It appeared that the suggestion received favourable approval of the Committee.[6]

The Flag Committee, after examining all the suggestions, finally came up with an entirely new design in August 1931. 'It suggested an entirely saffron flag with a brown *charkha* embellishing the upper quadrant.'

The new flag recommended by the Flag Committee failed to generate a consensus amongst the members of the CWC. There were no takers of the proposed design. Firstly, the flag was a complete departure from the *Swaraj*

13 *Jawaharlal Nehru.*

14 *The colour of the* Swaraj *flag on the label is similar to that of the flags of* 15 *Persia,* 16 *Mexico,* 17 *Bulgaria and* 18 *Italy. The similarity with Bulgaria is particularly striking.*

19 *T. Ramaswami Chowdary.*

20 *Madan Mohan Malaviya.*

20

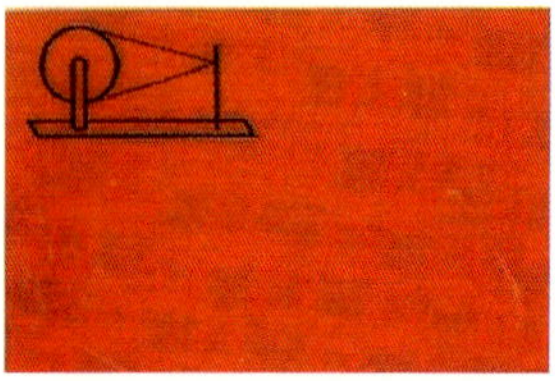

②①

flag then in vogue. Secondly, it was apprehended that the suggested colour would only help to intensify sentiments of isolation not only among Muslims but also within the grassroot level of the Congress and other communities. Hence, the final recommendation of the Flag Committee was instantly turned down by the CWC. Therefore, the new 'all-saffron flag' recommended by the Committee, never saw the light of day. As a result, the quest for a consensus on a new flag began all over again.

②① *The 'all-saffron' flag.*

Endnotes:

1. *The Encyclopaedia of the Indian National Congress*, 1921-24, vol. 8 (New Delhi: 1980), p.164.
2. G.V. Subha Rao, *Genesis of the Chakra Flag* (Goshti Book House, 1953), pp. 3–4.
3. Lt. Cdr. K.V. Singh, *Our National Flag* (New Delhi: Publications Division, 1991), pp. 57–58.
4. Ibid.
5. Vide Appendix III.
6. A complete list of sixty-four suggestions received by the Flag Committee can be found in the Nehru Memorial Museum and Library, New Delhi, AICC Papers, file no. 58.

The Purna Swaraj Flag

The CWC met in Bombay from 6 to 8 August 1931 and rejected the all-saffron flag model recommended by the Flag Committee on the grounds that it was politically unsuitable and also because the flag reflected a drastic change from the prevailing *Swaraj* flag.

The CWC, presided over by Sardar Vallabhbhai Patel, was attended by Mahatma Gandhi, Sarojini Naidu, Jawaharlal Nehru, Dr M.A. Ansari, Dr Syed Mohammed, Sardul Singh Caveeshar, J.M. Sen Gupta and Dr M.S. Aney. Jairamdas Daulatram, Abul Kalam Azad, Madan Mohan Malaviya, P. Sitaramayya, T.A.K. Sherwani and Purushottamdas Tandon were members co-opted.

Together they came up with a new tricolour design, named *Purna Swaraj* flag by substituting saffron for red and rearranging the disposition of the

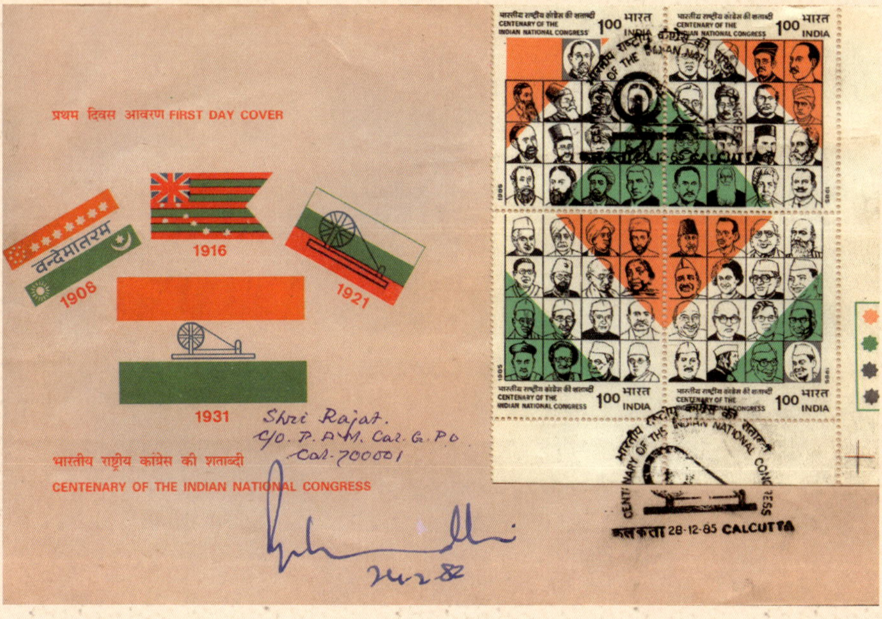

②

colours of the existing *Swaraj* flag. The new arrangement was in conformity with the basic principle of flag designing. Saffron over white over green with a *charkha* (spinning wheel) in navy blue at the centre of the white stripe. Since the colour white was interposed between saffron and green, all the three colours stood out distinctly from each other in the new flag. It implied that the colours stood for qualities not communities. The saffron would represent courage and sacrifice, white would stand for peace and truth, and green would symbolise faith and chivalry while the spinning wheel would be an emblem of hope of the masses.

③

Once the new flag was approved, Dr N.S. Hardikar, secretary of Hindustan Seva Dal, took the task of transferring the design of the flag onto cloth. Initially the flag, reportedly, had the 'spindle' of the *charkha* towards the flagstaff, but later the position of the *charkha* was altered to depict it towards the fly-end.

④

The endeavour to portray the evolution of *Swadeshi* flags in the FDC (see illustration 2) released on the occasion of the centenary of the Indian National Congress in 1985 had many inaccuracies. Due to the imperfect knowledge of the designer, Madame

⑤

Cama's flag was distorted to an extent. For instance the flag had 'eight lotuses' not 'seven stars and a dotted circle at the extreme left of the row'. Besides, the date label '1908' is factually wrong; the flag first appeared in 1907. Also, the Home Rule flag introduced in 1917 (not in 1916) is depicted without the crescent and star on the upper fly.

When Mahatma Gandhi was arrested on 4 January 1932 by the orders of Lord Wellington, the then British viceroy of India, a protest march was organised in Tirupur on 10 January. Tirupur Kumaran was leading the procession, holding the *Swaraj* flag in his hand, when police attacked Kumaran brutally. He exhibited an exemplary act of defiance against the police violence by holding the *Swaraj* flag up and kept chanting *'Vande Mataram'*. Next day, 11 January 1932, he breathed his last. He is known as *'kodi kaatha Kumaran'*—Kumaran who protected the flag.

Quit India movement, 1942

On 8 August 1942, Mahatma Gandhi gave the historic 'Quit India' call at the AICC session in Bombay.

> Here is the mantra, a short one that I give you. You may imprint it on your hearts and let every breath of yours give expression to it. The mantra is "Do or Die". We shall either free

① Sardar Vallabhbhai Patel described by the postmark as the 'architect of integrated India'.

② The se-tenant stamps show the profiles of all Congress presidents since the party's formation. The FDC is personally autographed by the Congress President Rajiv Gandhi who is also featured in one of the stamps.

③ Dr N.S. Hardikar.

④ 'Kumaran's hand holding the flag.' Postmark from Tirupur issued on 15 August 1997 to commemorate the 50th anniversary of Independence.

⑤ 'Tirupur Kumaran' postmark issued from Chennai defacing a stamp commemorating the martyr from Tirupur.

⑥ AICC Quit India Resolution, August 1942 stamp.

⑥

(7)

India or die in the attempt. We shall not live to see the perpetuation of our slavery.[1]

On 9 August 1942, following the arrest of most of the prominent leaders, Aruna Asaf Ali (Ganguli), came forward and unfurled the *Purna Swaraj* flag at the Gowalia Tank Maidan to announce the commencement of the Quit India movement. The raising of the flag by Aruna Asaf Ali provided the spark that ignited the Quit India movement. She became an iconic figure for thousands of youths who rose to emulate her. Forty-five years later, on 9 August 1987, Aruna Asaf Ali reenacted the flag hoisting ceremony at the same venue in Bombay, renamed August Kranti Maidan, to celebrate the fortieth anniversary of India's Independence.

(8)

The Quit India movement brought forth a host of volunteers and martyrs who performed great deeds of courage, heroism and sacrifice. The *Purna Swaraj* flag was declared outlawed but volunteers appeared all over the country and defied the order.

The city of Patna witnessed a memorable but heart-rending scene on 11 August 1942 that saw seven brave young students die and several others seriously injured by the bullets of the police in the campus of the old Patna Secretariat. These boys were raising anti-British slogans and were determined to hoist the *Purna Swaraj* flag on top of the Secretariat building.

(9)

The seven students whose names are engraved on the Martyrs' Memorial in Patna were:

Umakant Prasad Sinha	Ram Mohan Roy Seminary, class IX
Ramanand Singh	Ram Mohan Roy Seminary, class IX
Satish Prasad Jha	Patna Collegiate School, class X
Jalpati Kumar	Bihar National College, 2nd year
Devipada Choudhry	Miller High English School, class IX
Rajendra Singh	Patna High English School, Matriculation class
Ramgovind Singh	Punpun High English School, Matriculation class

(7) *'Do or Die Mahatma Gandhi': stamps remembering the Quit India movement led by Gandhi. The postmark issued from Calcutta depicts the* Purna Swaraj *flag.*

(8) *Aruna Asaf Ali. The postmark shows her waving the* Purna Swaraj *flag.*

(9) *The bronze sculpture by Debi Prasad Roychoudhury depicts the seven students who lost their lives while attempting to hoist the flag atop old Patna Secretariat building.*

(10) *Matangini Hazra statue, Kolkata.*

Se-tenant stamps (see illustration 11) were issued in 2002 to honour Matangini Hazra to mark the 60th anniversary of the Quit India movement and the formation of Tamluk national government.

Matangini Hazra was known as *'Gandhi-buri'* (literally an old female version of Gandhi). At the age of seventy-three she joined the Quit India movement, as an active volunteer. On 29 September 1942, while she was leading a procession at Tamluk in Midnapore, with the *Purna Swaraj* flag in her hands, a shower of bullets from the police felled her. While dying, she had held the flag high and had collapsed only when she had passed the flag onto the next marcher; the flag had remained unsullied.

(10)

11

12

The August Kranti (August Revolution) at Ballia in Uttar Pradesh, under the leadership of Chittu Pandey, was a stirring episode of the Quit India movement.

The *Purna Swaraj* flag had acquired overwhelming influence during the Quit India movement. Waving of the flag symbolised an act of defiance, as well as, a kind of proclamation of freedom.

Indian National Army (INA) Flag

Netaji Subhas Chandra Bose as the Supreme Commander of the Indian National Army (INA) better known as Azad Hind Fouz, adopted the *Purna Swaraj* flag by substituting the *charkha* with the 'springing tiger' in 1943. The springing tiger on the flag of the INA symbolised the strength of the Indian people and their indomitable will to fight. Interestingly, the springing tiger was also Tipu Sultan's emblem of revolt against the British.

①③

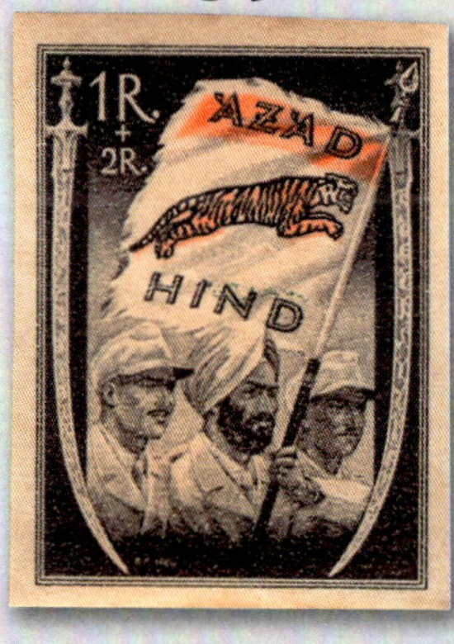

①④

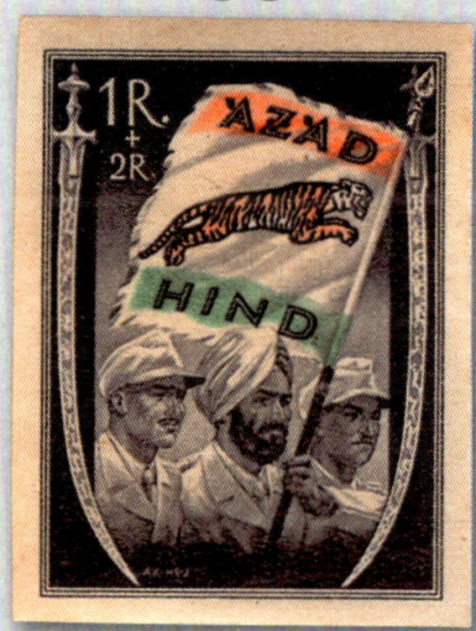

①⑤

These stamps were printed in 1943 at Reichsdruckerei, Berlin. The stamps were designed by the team consisting of Werner and Maria von Axter-Heudtlass. These stamps were never sent to India for postal service. Three types of semi-postal stamps in the denominations of '1R. + 2R.' are known to exist. According to S.A. Ayer, former minister of publicity of the provisional government of Azad Hind, 'Under Netaji's specific instructions a number of designs for stamps to be issued in the name of Azad Hind were prepared. Many of the designs were personally approved by Netaji.'[2] Biren Roy, Member of the Indian Parliament in 1968 said, 'I have spoken to Colonel of the INA Prem Saigal who was Netaji's private aide-de-camp in the Far East. He stated that the stamps were printed under the orders of Netaji Bose in Germany.'[3]

The Japanese sieged and held the Andaman and Nicobar Islands during World War II from March 1942 to October 1945. Netaji Subhas Bose paid a three-day visit to the islands as the head of the provisional government of India in December 1943. Netaji hoisted the Indian tricolour at the Gymkhana ground, Port Blair on 30 December 1943 for the first time. He renamed the Andaman and Nicobar Islands as 'Swaraj' and 'Shaheed

①① *Se-tenant stamps commemorating sixty years since Quit India movement; stamp on right depicting Matangini Hazra.*

①② *The August Kranti at Ballia.*

①③, ①④, ①⑤ *Never-issued postage stamps of Azad Hind Government* (National Indien).

①⑥ *This Indian postal stamp was issued in 1968 to commemorate the 25th anniversary of the founding of the provisional government of Azad Hind or Free India on 21 October 1943.*

①⑥

⑰

Dweep' (Martyr Island) respectively. However, the British forces recaptured the islands in October 1945.

On 14 April 1944, Colonel S.A. Malik, of the Bahadur group of the INA, raised the flag of freedom for the first time on Indian soil at Moirang, about forty-five kilometres from Imphal in Manipur after defeating the British forces there.

⑱

Sheel Bhadra Yajee, a close associate of Netaji, was actively associated with the INA movement and carried on the onerous task of implementing instructions to assist the INA in the ongoing struggle in Nagaland and Manipur in Netaji's absence. After Indian Independence, Sheel Bhadra was instrumental in the construction of the INA Martyrs Memorial at Moirang. The Memorial was unveiled by V.V. Giri, the former president of India in 1968.

When the fortunes of the war turned, the INA had to finally surrender to the Allies in August 1945. Netaji disappeared from the scene while on his last-known flight from Saigon. After the final surrender by the INA to the British forces in South East Asia, the British government decided to try for sedition a large number of INA soldiers who had actually fought for the country's freedom.

Delhi's Red Fort (Lal Quila), where the INA dreamt to march with flying colours, became the stage for their own trials on charges of treason. The first trial began in 1945 with three senior officers of the INA: Col. Prem Sahgal, Col. Gurubaksh Singh and Major General Shah Nawaz Khan. The chargesheet against the accused was 'waging war against His Majesty the King-Emperor'. The Congress set up an INA Defence Committee which consisted of such eminent lawyers as Bhulabhai Desai, Tej Bahadur Sapru, Kailashnath Katju and Asaf Ali. Nehru was a member of the Committee. A great sense of drama gripped the nation as these national leaders stood up to defend the INA officers in the historic hall of Delhi's Red Fort. The court martial held all accused to be guilty and they were convicted.[4] These trials generated much publicity and public sympathy for the defendants who were perceived as true patriots. Disenchantment also began to surface amongst a section of the Indian members in the various establishments of the armed forces. It marked the high point of solidarity between the Congress, Muslim and Communists ranks. In January 1946, naval officers, demanding the release of INA men, put up a collective display of Congress, League and red flags on their ships. The INC and the All India Muslim League made 'the release of the INA prisoners' a major political issue. The *Purna Swaraj* flag and the green flag of the

19

17 Netaji Subhas Chandra Bose. Port Blair postmark.

18 Sheel Bhadra Yajee.

19 The Red Fort and INA officers: Prem Sahgal, G.S. Dhillon and Shah Nawaz Khan.

②⓪

Muslim League were flown together at protests. Thus it became a significant turning point in the history of events during the final phase of the struggle for Independence.

A patriotic envelope (see illustration 20) was posted during World War II (11 December 1940 to be precise) from Singapore, then part of the Straits Settlements. It shows the portrait of Mahatma Gandhi flanked by *Purna Swaraj* flags. It has the legend *'Bande Mataram'* printed in Tamil. The registered envelope was opened and its contents were censored by the British authorities prior to its transmission.

②①

The *Purna Swaraj* flag was used extensively on propaganda leaflets (see illustration 21) in the far east, distributed by the Indian Independence League volunteers during the early phase of World War II.

②⓪ *An envelope with patriotic emblems.*

②① *The* Purna Swaraj *flag on a propaganda leaflet.*

Endnotes:

1. P.N. Chopra, *Quit India Movement* (New Delhi: Publications Division, 1987), p. 9.
2. Herbert A. Friedman, *"Azad Hind" and "Chalo Delhi" Stamps* (Bombay: Jal Cooper, 1972), p. 12.
3. Ibid.
4. Barun De, *Freedom Struggle* (New Delhi: National Book Trust, 1994), p. 217.

Free India's National Flag

On 20 February 1947, the British Prime Minister, Clement Attlee, announced that they would transfer all powers to India definitely by June 1948. Accordingly, Lord Louis Mountbatten, the last Viceroy of India worked out a compromise between the Congress and the Muslim League and brought forward the date of transfer of power to 15 August 1947.

The day, 15 August 1947, was of historic significance. Exactly two years earlier, on 15 August 1945, the surrender of Japan was announced, signalling the end of World War II.

①

②

① London SW1 postmark dated 2 November 1983, issued to commemorate the unveiling of Mountbatten's statue in London honouring Admiral of the Fleet, the Earl Mountbatten of Burma, who, as Supreme Commander South East Asia Allied Forces, accepted the surrender of Japan in Singapore.

② Souvenir, 'Day of Surrender. 15 August 1945.' Japan's surrender marks the end of World War II.

③

Prior to India's Independence, the Constituent Assembly set up a nine-member ad hoc committee on 23 June 1947 to recommend a new flag for Independent India.

The members of the ad hoc committee were Dr Rajendra Prasad (Chairman), Abul Kalam Azad, C. Rajagopalachari, Sarojini Naidu, K.M. Pannikkar, K.M. Munshi, B.R. Ambedkar, S.N. Gupta, Frank Anthony and Sardar Ujjal Singh.

Lord Mountbatten put forward a proposal on 24 June 1947 to the Congress and Muslim League leaders to retain the 'Union Jack' at the canton of the national flags of the dominions of India and Pakistan respectively, to reflect the symbolic continuity with Britain, but his proposal failed to garner enough support from most of the leaders and was eventually turned down.

Regarding the protest against the viceroy's proposal to include a small Union Jack in the Indian flag, *The Hindu* on 19 July 1997 reported that Gandhi had remarked, 'Nothing wrong in that as long as India was a Dominion included in the British Commonwealth. Such a display would be an act of courtesy, and a gesture worthy of the best traditions built up in India.' But he had learnt at the CWC meeting that the Union Jack was not, in fact, going to be included in the flag. Gandhi asked his audience not to rejoice over this omission!

④

V.D. Savarkar sent a telegram from Bombay to Dr Rajendra Prasad, Dr B.R. Ambedkar, Sardar Vallabhbhai Patel and Dr N.B. Khare on 7 July 1947, reading thus:

> 'The standard of Hindustan must be Bhagwa-ochre coloured (.) the Charkha too must be replaced by a Chakra - wheel - or any other symbol signifying progress and strength.'[1]

S.D. Kalelkar, hailing from Nagpur, in an article titled 'Thoughtful Suggestion', published in the *Harijan* on 6 July 1947, suggested a simple wheel in place of the *charkha*, making it easier to draw it symmetrically on the flag.

The ad hoc flag committee finally referred to the strong sentiment in the country in favour of adopting the *Purna Swaraj* flag used for years as the national flag of India and suggested that it should be duly honoured. After detailed deliberations the committee decided on 14 July to retain the *Purna Swaraj* flag by replacing the *charkha* emblem with Asoka's Dharma Chakra (Wheel of Law) at the centre of the white stripe.

The flag committee immediately arranged for the samples of the new flag for approval. The sample prepared by Mrs Badr-ud-Din Tyabji was approved unanimously on 17 July 1947. (Her husband was the joint secretary in the Constituent Assembly and grandson of the great Tyabji who was the president of the Congress party in 1887.) It was then decided that Pandit Jawaharlal Nehru would place the recommendations before the Constituent Assembly on 22 July 1947.

⑤

⑥

③ *Dr Rajendra Prasad.*

④ *This 1s 6d stamp marking the Gandhi birth centenary year (1969), is a first of its kind from Great Britain to commemorate a foreign leader and also the first to be designed by a foreign artist—Biman Mullick.*

⑤ *A cartoon by* The Indian Express *cartoonist Gopi, in the issue of 17 July 1947, captured the nationwide mood at that time.*

⑥ *V.D. Savarkar.*

The wheel on the *chakra* flag is intimately linked to Indian heritage and tradition. It is a reflection of India's religious beliefs, philosophical convictions and universal popular beliefs. The twenty-four spokes,

> … stand for the twenty-four modes of principal casual relations spoken in Buddhist philosophy. As a whole, it represents the Wheel of Law which is considered the king of kings and whose message of righteousness was binding even on the greatest monarch.[2]

⑦

Gandhi was not too happy with the replacement of the *charkha* in the flag with Asoka's Dharma Chakra. Though Nehru insisted that the change was not significant, Gandhi had his reservations, fearing that the association with the lion in the Asokan emblem would signify violence. He admitted in a statement published in the *Harijan* that, 'Nothing would have lost (sic) if our councillors had never thought of interfering with the design of the original flag.'[3] In a statement made in Lahore on 6 August 1947, subsequently quoted in *The Statesman* a couple of days later, Gandhi said,

> I must say that, if the Flag of the Indian Union will not embody the emblem of the *Charkha*, I will refuse to salute that flag. You know the National Flag of India was first thought of by me, and I cannot conceive of India's National Flag without the emblem of the *Charkha*. We have, however been told by Pandit Nehru and others that the sign of the Wheel or *Chakra* in the National flag symbolises the *Charkha* also...

The decision to remove the *charkha* evoked mixed reactions outside the Constituent Assembly. A correspondent from Hyderabad declared, 'Gandhiji is being buried alive.' Citing some of the speeches of the Constituent Assembly debate to illustrate his stand, he further wrote, 'The new wheel or Asokan chakra has no connection with Gandhi's

8

wheel; wheel is the sign of "non-violent economy" while the new one represents the Sudarshan chakra, which represents violence.'[4] Gandhi himself was very upset about the substitution of the *chakra* for the *charkha* but he gradually came around to the view that the *chakra* of the flag was the Asokan Chakra and not the Sudarshan Chakra. He also admitted that the notion of the Sudarshan Chakra as a symbol of violence was a popular misconception. He however maintained, 'if we neglect the charkha ...we will be acting like a man who remembers God in sorrow and forgets him when he showers happiness.'[5]

7 Gandhi on se-tenant postage stamps.

8 Gandhi and world leaders of the twentieth century honoured by Antigua and Barbuda by issuing postage stamps depicting their respective national flags.

9, 10, 11, 12 Gandhi and the national flag depicted on a selection of stamps issued by different countries.

9

10

11

12

13

14

15

As had been decided earlier, Pandit Nehru moved the resolution for adoption of the new national flag recommended by the ad hoc committee at the Constituent Assembly on 22 July 1947.

The Constituent Assembly Debates of 22 July 1947

With Dr Rajendra Prasad in the Chair, Pandit Nehru delivered the opening speech after moving the resolution on the new national flag, the 'Flag of Independent India':

16

> Resolved that the National flag of India shall be a horizontal tricolour of deep saffron (kesari), white and dark green in equal proportion. In the centre of the white band, there shall be a wheel in navy blue to represent the charkha. The design of the wheel shall be that of the wheel (chakra) which appears on the Sarnath lion capital of Asoka. The diameter of the wheel shall approximate to the width of the white band. The ratio of the width to the length of the flag shall ordinarily be 2:3.[6]

The Hindustan Times on 23 July 1947 reported the day's proceedings under the heading 'Flag of Independent India':

17

18

19

13 *Stamps commemorating Nehru's birthday and birth centenary with the national flag as the backdrop.*

14, 15 *The stamps issued to commemorate the* Swatantra Bharat, *a Hindi daily from Lucknow, depicts the first page of the newspaper's first issue dated 15 August 1947. The lead photograph shows Jawaharlal Nehru presenting the national flag to the Constituent Assembly on 22 July 1947.*

16, 17, 18, 19 *Nehru and the national flag depicted on a selection of stamps issued by various countries.*

The Indian constituent Assembly today unanimously adopted the tricolor as the National flag of India. All members without exception stood up for half a minute in solemn silence to pass the resolution and to pay homage to the Flag of the Nation. ... The proceedings excelled the expectation of everyone by the warmth, patriotic emotion and unanimity. Pandit Nehru's speech was couched in words befitting the great occasion and some thought that no more speeches were necessary. But the House felt otherwise. The House demanded that full opportunity should be given to members to speak on the occasion. As one member said: *"A nation adopts its Flag only once. Let us have our say"*. It became a 'National Flag Day' in the Constituent Assembly.

The amendment notices served earlier were also immediately withdrawn in favour of the flag presented by Pandit Nehru.

H.V. Kamath who had urged that the swastika, the ancient Indian symbol of *'satyam, shivam, sundaram'* (truth is eternal and beautiful), be

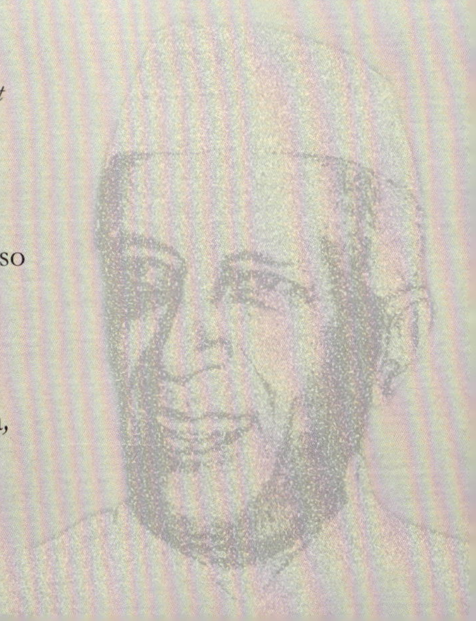

inscribed on the wheel, withdrew his amendment notice by saying that when he had sent in the amendment, he had done so without seeing the design of the flag. Upon seeing the flag now, he begged the House to excuse him since he no longer wanted to press for the amendment.

20

Dr P.B. Deshmukh also withdrew his amendment notice by announcing that after Pandit Nehru's speech, pregnant with emotion and significance, one is diffident about adding anything further that may be misconstrued as a criticism of the speech. Hence he did not wish to move the amendment, although he maintained that his idea did hold some worth.

The House particularly welcomed the speech made in Hindustani by the leader of the Muslim League, Chaudhry Khaliquzzaman. He declared that from this day onwards, every citizen of India, irrespective of the religion he may belong to, will make sacrifices to defend the dignity and honour of this flag. He urged the people of India to forget its bitter past in recent times and to make a fresh start with sincerity, dignity and willingness in order to rebuild the country. Though a flag is merely a piece of cloth, Khaliquzzaman stated that this hoisted flag will be looked upon with great pride, honour and patriotism across India.

21

PAKISTAN پاکستان

22

Dr Sarvepalli Radhakrishnan in his speech echoed the views advanced by Prof. Suniti Chatterji (*The National Flag*) and interpreted the colours of the flag in philosophical terms. He said that the colour green is symbolic of mankind's relationship with soil, plant life and nature. Man has to create his paradise on this green planet. To successfully complete this venture man must be guided by truth (symbolised by the colour white), be virtuous (symbolised by the wheel), practise self-control and embrace renunciation (symbolised by the colour saffron). Ultimately the flag's message is one of unity. Men belonging to different faiths should come together to build a democratic republic with freedom of expression, compassion and flexibility.

Frank R. Anthony explained the role he had played as a member of the ad hoc committee that gave shape to this flag. He wanted it to be clear that this flag did not have communal overtones. He also emphasised that the committee had essentially retained the design of the flag that had been at

23

20 Dr. P.B. Deshmukh.

21 Leader of the Muslim League, Chaudhry Khaliquzzaman.

22 Issued on Dr Radhakrishnan's retirement as President of India in 1967. A very rare honour for a person to be depicted on a postage stamp during his own lifetime. The cover was personally autographed by Dr Radhakrishnan.

23 Frank R. Anthony.

the forefront of India's freedom struggle and eventual victory. He further asserted that the traits and motives embedded in this national flag are values that should be dear to every nation that wants to embrace the road to freedom and progress.

Giani Gurmukh Singh Musafir felt that after the speeches of great men such as Pandit Jawaharlal Nehru and Dr Radhakrishnan, who had so brilliantly interpreted the colours of the flag, there was no need for him to talk at length. However, on behalf of the Sikh community he assured the House that the Sikhs would continue to uphold the honour of the flag by making the kind of sacrifices and showing the undaunted fortitude reflected during India's freedom struggle.

㉔

Rev. Jerome D'Souza thanked the members for giving him the opportunity to be a part of the chorus of expressing happiness on the very auspicious occasion, when India, without distinction of religion, caste or creed, province or section accepted a national emblem. He reminded the House of the historic occasion when this very building was inaugurated by the then Viceroy General, Lord Irwin. Lord Irwin, alluding to the circular construction of the building had quoted a great English poet, by saying that he had seen 'eternity as a circle of white light'. Rev. Jerome D'Souza compared this circle with the wheel on the flag, saying that it represents time and its onslaughts, industry, eternity and the values associated with eternal life.

㉕

Lakshmi Narayan Sahu said that when he beheld the colours of the flag, he was reminded of the three idols in the Jagannath temple in Puri. Lord Jagannath stands for the colour blue, while Balaram and Subhadra Devi stand for white and yellow, respectively. Jagannath and Balaram shielding and protecting Subhadra Devi on either side signifies their stance of defending women.

Mrs Sarojini Naidu, the *'Bulbule Hind'*, was given the honour of making the final speech. She concluded her long emotional speech by stating

②⑥

②⑦

that as a poet and a woman she was speaking in prose when emphasising that the women of India symbolise the unity of the nation. She reminded those present that this national flag would not differentiate between the rich and the poor. Further, this flag would not bestow any privilege; rather it would expect responsible behaviour and sacrifice. Hindus, Muslims, Christians, Sikhs, Zoroastrians and others may belong to different religions but they are one in the undivided heart of Mother India. Finally, she urged the regenerated spirit of India to salute the national flag.

Other speakers who took part in the debate and spoke on the occasion but have not yet been philatelically honoured are: H.V. Kamath, Seth Govind Das, V.I. Muniswami Pillai, Dr Mohan Singh Mehta, Mohamed Sheriff, Satyanarayan Sinha, Tejamul Hussain, B.K. Sidwa, Pandit Govind Malaviya, Balkrishna Sharma, Saiyid Mohammed Saadullah, Dr H.C. Mukherjee, R.K. Sidwa, H.J. Khandekar, Joseph Alban D'Souza, Jai Narayan Vyas, S. Nagappa and Lakshmi Narayan Sahu.

②④ *Giani Gurmukh Singh Musafir.*

②⑤ *Rev. Jerome D'Souza.*

②⑥ *Rathayatra at Puri, the site of the famous Jagannath temple.*

②⑦ *Mrs Sarojini Naidu, the* 'Bulbule Hind'.

28

29

The cotton-khadi flag, which was unfurled by Pandit Nehru on 22 July 1947 in the Constituent Assembly, is held as the 'standard flag' in the custody of the Chief Inspector, Chief Inspectorate of Textiles and Clothing, Kanpur.

Homage to the Indian National Flag

O lovely dawn of freedom that breaks in gold and purple over the ancient capital of Prithviraj!
O splendid flag of newborn India to be unfurled on the morrow over the Red Fort of Shahjehan!
We pay you the homage of our dedicated heart and hands
And pledge ourselves to translate into glorious deeds
The dreams that were our share and inspiration in the long darkness of our bondage.

—Sarojini Naidu, *The Statesman*, 15 August 1947.

National Flag atop Council House (Parliament Bhavan)

At the stroke of midnight on 15 August 1947, free India's national flag was hoisted atop the Council House, renamed Parliament Bhavan in New Delhi. The flag was presented by Mrs Hansa Mehta representing the Flag Presentation Committee, comprising all the women members of the Constituent Assembly, as a gift from the women of India.

30

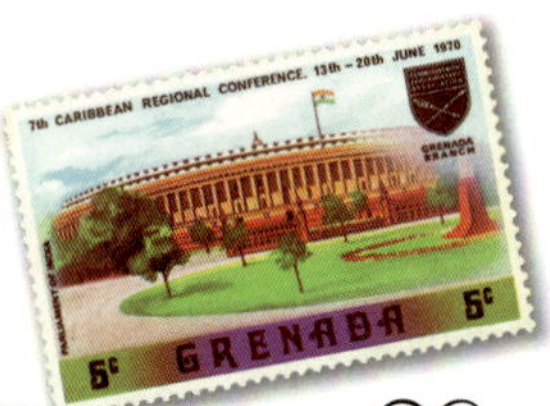

31

32

33

34

35

28 Jawaharlal Nehru with national flag.

29 Homage to the Indian national flag.

30, 31, 32 Indian national flag atop Parliament House.

33 'A bare flag-pole' atop Parliament Bhavan, the 50-rupees currency note introduced in 1975.

34 'The flag-pole with flag in position', 50-rupees currency note as modified in 1980.

35 Revised 50-rupees currency note introduced on 14 March 1997.

15TH AUGUST 1947

36

37

38

On 15 August 1947, during the swearing-in-ceremony at the Viceroy's House re-named 'Government House', the new government took the oath and independent India's flag was raised for the first time on the central dome at 10:30 am.

The standard of the Viceroy of India came down the flagstaff of the Viceroy's House for the last time on the evening of 14 August 1947. The historic flag is now preserved in the Norman Abbey of Romsey, the last viceroy's parish church in England.

In the Residency of Lucknow, the Union Jack was hauled down for the last time about twenty-four hours before the transfer of power from British to Indian hands on 14 August 1947. The hauling-down programme was kept a well-guarded secret by the British military authorities.

39

40

41

42

The Lucknow Residency witnessed the scene of a bloody event during the uprising in 1857, known in Britain as the Sepoy Mutiny and in India as the First War of Independence, sparked by the court martial of Indian sepoys (soldiers) who refused on religious grounds to use rifle cartridges greased with animal fat.

Throughout the siege of the Lucknow Residency, the Union Jack was kept flying on the tower, to signal any approaching relief column that the British still awaited. Even after the British forces suppressed the uprising, the Union Jack was kept flying on the flagstaff of the Residency. In the whole of the British Empire, when all flags were brought down at dusk, it was the only spot in the British Empire where the Union Jack was never lowered.

From August 1947 to January 1950, the governor general of India had a dark blue flag bearing the royal crest with a lion standing on a crown, beneath which was the word 'India' embroidered in gold.

A distinctive standard of the President of India was devised when the post of the 'governor general' was abolished and India became a

36 FDC: 'Nehru and Mountbatten.' The stamp features Mountbatten.

37 C. Rajagopalachari, the first Indian governor general of India was in office from 21 June 1948 to 26 January 1950.

38 Viceroy's House.

39 The standard of the governor general of India. This silk flag was issued by Kensitas Cigarettes as an advertising gimmick in 1934.

40 The Residency, Lucknow–a vintage postcard printed in Saxony.

41 Postage stamp issued in 2007 to commemorate the 150th anniversary of the First War of Independence, 1857.

43

44

Republic on 26 January 1950. The President's flag was flown from sunrise to sunset on the dome of Rashtrapati Bhavan until 1971. The flag consisted of four quadrants of blue and red with the emblems in gold: The lion capital of Asoka (third century BC) represents authority; the elephant has been taken from the Ajanta frescoes (fourth century) symbolising justice and equality. The scales, a seventeenth-century Moslem design from the Red Fort, Delhi, are symbols of equality and fraternity and the lotus bowl from Sarnath, (c. first century BC) represents peace and prosperity.

The President's standard fell into disuse in 1971. Since then it is the Indian national flag that flies on the dome of Rashtrapati Bhavan.

With the birth of the Indian Republic on 26 January 1950, the name 'Government House' was changed to Rashtrapati Bhavan. The Rashtrapati Bhavan is the official residence of the President of India. Until 1950 it served as the residence of the viceroy and governor general of India. At present, it is the largest residence of any chief of state in the world.

First Public Flag Salutation Ceremony

The first public flag salutation ceremony was held in the afternoon of 15 August 1947 near the War Memorial Arch, later renamed India Gate. As the Prime Minister unfurled the flag against a clear blue sky, a rainbow resembling the hues of the flag appeared out of the blue on the horizon which startled the crowd that had assembled there.

The *Asian Age* on 16 February 1997, featured an article where Lord Mountbatten, the last viceroy and the first constitutional governor general of India, had recorded the events of 15 August 1947 a day after they occurred.

④⑤

④⑥

> At 6 p.m. the great event of the day was to take place – the salutation of the new Dominion flag. This programme had originally included a ceremonial lowering of the Union Jack. But when I discussed this with Nehru he entirely agreed that this was a day they wanted everybody to be happy, and if the lowering of the Union Jack in any way offended British susceptibilities he would certainly see that it did not take place, the more so as the Union Jack would still be flown on certain days in the Dominion, such as the King's birthday.

It was the most remarkable day of his life, recalled Lord Mountbatten,

> As the flag broke a brilliant rainbow appeared in the sky, which was taken by the whole crowd as a good omen. (I had never noticed how closely a rainbow could resemble the new Dominion flag of saffron, white and green.)

Prime Minister Nehru unfurled the national flag for the first time on the ramparts of the Red Fort on 16 August 1947 at 8:30 am. On this occasion, Nehru referred to Netaji Subhas Bose's call of *'Chalo Dilli'* (onward to Delhi) and his dream of hoisting the 'flag of freedom' atop Delhi's Red Fort.

However, since 1948, every year, the official Independence Day flag-hoisting ceremony is

④② Standard of the President of India, 1950–1971.

④③ The Rashtrapati Bhavan: a set of four stamps and a miniature sheet issued by India Post on 5 August 2011.

④④ The postmark shows the bare flag-mast (flag-mast without flag) on the central dome of Rashtrapati Bhavan.

④⑤, ④⑥ War Memorial Arch, New Delhi.

④⑦ The first public flag salutation at War Memorial Arch.

④⑦

④⑧

④⑨

performed on 15 August by the Indian Prime Minister's designate at the Red Fort.

Where are the first historic flags of free India?

National newspapers reported from time to time about the missing historic flags. The first flag was hoisted at the stroke of midnight on 15 August 1947 over the Council Hall; the second one was hoisted for public salutation at the War Memorial Gate on the next day (15 August) in the afternoon and the third one was hoisted at the Red Fort on the morning of 16 August 1947. But sixty-four years after Independence, no one knows for sure where they may be found. Following the media reports, searches to trace the flags at the National Archives of India, National Museum, Red Fort Museum, Nehru Memorial Museum and Library, Ministry of External Affairs Archives, Rashtrapati Bhavan Museum, Parliament Museum and in other likely places drew a complete blank till 2002 when it was claimed that the Red Fort flag had been discovered in the Officers' Mess Headquarter, Delhi Area. *The Sunday Pioneer* on 27 February 2011 came out with a piece claiming that they had found the hitherto untraced Red Fort flag. *The Pioneer* declared,

> The historic Red Fort flag is in the safe custody of the Indian Army, displayed prominently – encased in a frame - at the Army's Battle Honours Mess at Delhi. Not just that, foreign dignitaries visiting the Mess are informed about the legacy of the flag, which rightfully occupies the most prominent place in the Mess.

(The veracity of the report is yet to be confirmed, in view of earlier statements made by the army spokesperson about their ignorance regarding the whereabouts of the flag.)

Hyderabad's reluctance to hoist the national flag

The Nizam of Hyderabad declared that the Hyderabad state would remain a sovereign power and would not join either India or Pakistan after the transfer of power. *The Telegraph* on 15 August 1997 stated that it was declared in Hyderabad that on 15 August 1947, 'No flag of any foreign state shall be ceremoniously flown in any public meeting nor any salutation of such flag be made.' Any contravention of the ban would be punishable with imprisonment and fine or both. The newspaper quoted Swami Ramanand Teerth, the then state Congress President saying, 'We should not consider the Indian Union flag as that of any foreign state. We wish Hyderabad to be part and parcel of the Indian Union.' Finally, as a gesture of compromise, the Indian tricolour and the Nizam's *Asufiyah* flag were hoisted together atop the Telegraph office of the Indian Government alongside the Residency building, at exactly one minute after the stroke of midnight on 15 August 1947.

Md. Ismail Sahib, President of the Madras Provincial Muslim League called upon all Muslims in the Madras province to celebrate Independence Day on 15 August 1947, by hoisting the Indian national flag.

Postal recognition of Independent India

The first postal reference to Independent India occurred on 15 August 1947, in the form of a commemorative postmark inscribed with the slogan *'Jai Hind'* in Devanagari and Roman scripts. The *'Jai Hind'* postmark continued to be used for cancelling mails for a considerable period of time in the major post offices of India.

50

51

48 The Indian flag with the Red Fort in the background.

49 Se-tenant stamps honouring the martyrs issued on 15 August 1998.

50 Swami Ramanand Teerth.

52

51 Md. Ismail Sahib.

52 The 'Jai Hind' postmark.

53

The Department of Posts and Telegraphs, as it was known then, failed to bring out a suitable postage stamp acceptable to the authority to commemorate the historic day of India's Independence. There exists an unissued 'essay' of the commemorative stamp (see illustration 54) which was prepared hastily but not approved by the concerned authority.

54

The first post-Independence postage stamp of India was issued on 21 November 1947 (the date '15 Aug 1947' inscribed on the stamp is a misnomer). The stamp portrays the national flag and has the slogan *'Jai Hind'* in Devanagari script (see illustration 53).

55

56

57

53 First post-Independence postage stamps of India.

54 Unissued 'essay' of stamps to commemorate India's Independence.

55 Official 'flag logo' for the commemoration of the 50th anniversary of India's Independence, 1947-1997.

56 Official 'flag logo' for the celebration of 'Forty years of Freedom 1947-1987'.

57 'Freedom Forty—Swaraj'. The postmark dated 16 August 1988, depicts the facsimile of the first post-Independence postage stamp of India.

Endnotes:

1. P. Thankappan Nair, *Indian National Songs and Symbols* (Firma KLM, 1987), p. 109.
2. C. Sivaramamurti, *Our National Emblem* (New Delhi: Publications Division, 1966), p. 8.
3. Arundhati Virmani, 'From Charkha To Chakra', *The Sunday Statesman*, 10 August 1997.
4. M.K. Gandhi, *The Collected Works of Mahatma Gandhi*, vol. 89 (New Delhi: Publications Division, 1976), p. 120.
5. Ibid., p. 484.
6. 'The Constituent Assembly of India Debates, Volume IV.' See: http://www.indiankanoon.org/doc/21455/

Famous Flag-Related Events

Flags are interpretative symbols. Achievements in the fields of expeditions, scientific explorations and adventure sports, etc., are symbolically proclaimed by hoisting appropriate flags and banners.

Conquest of Mount Everest, 1953

Planting the flag mounted on an ice axe atop the conquered peak is a typical mountaineering tradition across the world.

①

Darjeeling was the starting point of all expeditions before Nepal opened its doors to the outside world in the early 1950s. Tenzing Norgay waved his ice axe bearing the flags of the United Nations, Great Britain, Nepal and India atop Mt. Everest for the first time on 29 May 1953 at 11:30 am. The design of the postmark (see illustration 1) was adapted from the famous photograph taken by fellow summiteer Edmund Hillary.

The Indian national flag that was carried to the peak of Mt. Everest for the first time on 29 May 1953 is now on display at the Rashtrapati Bhavan Museum, New Delhi. Later, several other Indian mountaineers carried the Indian national flag to the top of the world.

②

Captain H.P.S. Ahluwalia and Phu Dorji of the Indian Mt. Everest Expedition (1965) proudly holding the Indian national flag at the summit on

29 May 1965, were featured on a commemorative stamp (see illustration 2). The picture on the stamp was taken by mountaineer Harish C.S. Rawat at 10:30 am when a high-speed westerly wind made the tricolour flutter atop Mt. Everest against a deep blue sky. For the first time three men stood together on the top of the world.

The Indian flag was very close to the summit during the conquest of Kanchenjunga in 1977 (see illustration 4). As promised earlier to the Sikkimese Lamas, the summiteers Major Prem Chand and Naik N.D. Sherpa, did not step on the summit but stopped six feet short of it.

① 50th anniversary of the conquest of Mt. Everest. Commemorative postmark issued from Darjeeling on 29 May 2004.

② Captain H.P.S. Ahluwalia and Phu Dorji of the Indian Mt. Everest Expedition, 1965.

③ New Zealand celebrated the 50th anniversary of the conquest of Mt. Everest.

④ Conquest of Kanchenjunga (8586 m), the highest mountain in India and the third highest in the world by the Indian Army Mountaineering Expedition on 31 May 1977.

Flags over the South Pole

On 9 January 1982, the first Indian Antarctic Expedition planted the Indian national flag, Indian naval ensign, air force and coast guard ensigns over Dakshin Gangotri, Antarctica.

⑤

India gained admittance to the Antarctic Treaty on 19 August 1983 and was given Consultative Status on 12 September 1983. India was inducted as a member of the Scientific Committee on Antarctic Research (SCAR) on 1 October 1984 and the Convention on the Conservation of Antarctic Marine Living Resources (CCAMLR) in 1986.

Indian flag in outer space

The Indian national flag was carried for the first time on the moon during the Apollo 15 mission between 26 July–7 August 1971. Apollo 15 became the ninth manned mission in the American Apollo space program and the fourth to land on the moon. Flags of all the United Nations member countries, each four by six inches in size, were carried on this mission and returned to earth.

⑥

Breakthroughs in space science and technology have become so common nowadays that astronautics has become an essential part of everyday life.

There are frequent collaborations between different countries for the exploration of outer space. Squadron leader Rakesh Sharma became the first Indian cosmonaut-explorer to orbit the earth in a joint USSR-India manned space mission under 'Inter-Cosmos Programme' on 3 April 1984.

⑦

The Indian national flag flew into space as a medallion adorning the space suit worn by Rakesh Sharma during the Indo-Soviet joint space flight. On 3 April 1984, when he was asked on air by the then Prime Minister of India, Indira Gandhi, to describe what India looked like from space, pat came his reply, *'Main binaa jhijhak ke keh sakta hoon, "Sare Jahan Se Achcha."'* (I can say without any hesitation, 'It is the best in the world.')[1]

⑧

⑤ The stamp was issued in 1983 to commemorate the first anniversary of the Indian Antarctic Expedition.

⑥ FDC personally autographed by the crew of the joint USSR-India space flight, 3–11 April 1984. By Yuri Malyshev, pilot-cosmonaut, ship's commander; Gennady Strekalov, pilot-cosmonaut, flight engineer and Rakesh Sharma, cosmonaut-explorer.

⑦ The miniature sheet issued by the then USSR shows the 'Cosmonauts aboard the Salyut 7 space station'.

⑧ Malagasy commemorates the India-USSR Inter-Cosmos space flight in 1985.

⑨

⑨ *'India in Space', se-tenant stamps issued on Children's Day, 14 November 2000.*

A painting by S. Praveen (see illustration 9), winner of the first prize in the senior category in stamp design competition for children held in 1999 on the theme 'India in Space – 2025'. Indicative of the fascination of the young mind for space exploration and the quest for knowledge about the unknown. It also brings out the yearning of the new generation to see India excelling.[2]

Endnotes:

1. A quote from Md. Iqbal's famous patriotic poem in Urdu.
2. Taken from the brochure published by Department of Posts, India, issued along with the above stamps.

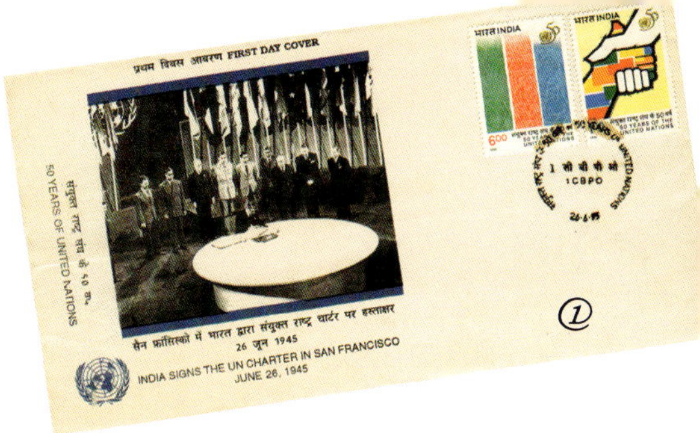

Uses of Flags: International Forums

Freedom is heralded by hoisting of a new national flag. Inclusion of that flag in front of the UN building in New York is the symbolic equivalent of being recognized as a real country.[1]

India signed the UN charter on 26 June 1945. The United Nations in its bid to mark the emergence of India as an independent country, held a flag-hoisting ceremony on 16 August 1947 where the old flag of British India was lowered and replaced by that of the new national flag of independent India in front of the main entrance of the Headquarters building, Lake Success, New York, where fifty-five flagpoles were arranged in a circle with the flags of all member nations.

① India signs the UN charter in San Francisco, 26 June 1945.

② This UN international generic personalised stamp sheet was issued in 2009. It shows the flags of the UN member nations at United Nations Headquarters with the Secretariat Building in the background (the photograph was taken in 1959).

According to the press release of the United Nations Postal Administration, the national flags on the 'Flag Series' stamps were to be identical to the flags flying outside the UN Headquarters. Achieving dimensional accuracy and true colour in the designs was such exacting work that it took months of work before the designs left the drawing board. But the final result of the Indian national flag (see illustration 9) shows the Asoka Chakra with twelve spokes, instead of the actual twenty-four spokes.

The first meeting of the Universal Postal Union (UPU) was held at Bern in 1874. India became a founder member of the UPU in 1876.

③

Apropos to the UN General Assembly resolution in 1950, India had sent an army medical mission for the UN Peacekeeping Force in the Korean War for the rear logistic support of the combat units (see illustration 10 and 11).

The first Afro-Asian conference of the newly independent states of Africa and Asia was held in Bandung, Indonesia in April 1955 (see illustration 12).

④

⑤

⑥

⑦

⑧

⑨

③ Flags of the UPU member nations. Postcard issued by San Marino in 1984 to commemorate the 19th Universal Postal Union Congress held in Hamburg, West Germany.

④, ⑤ 15th anniversary of Asian-Oceanic Postal Union (AOPU)–1977.

⑥ UN Conference for Technical Cooperation between Developing Countries (TCDC) in the domain of 'Education through Television'–1978.

⑦ UN Security Council (UNSC) Meeting, Addis Ababa–1972.

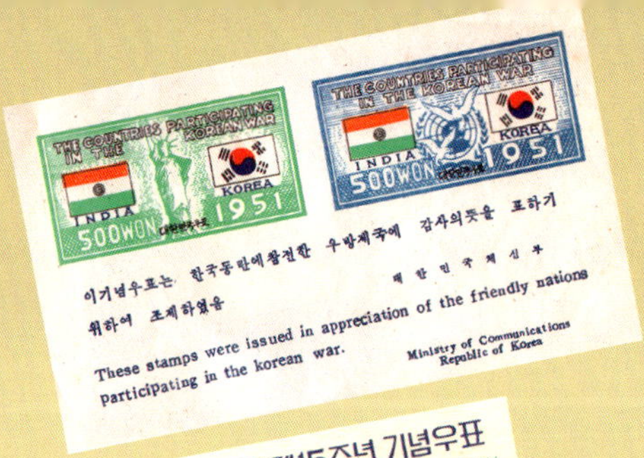

10

11

The post-World War II period saw the beginning of the Cold War confrontation and rivalry between the superpowers. It was at this juncture that the Non-Aligned Movement was forged, putting forth an alternative vision for the handling of international affairs and the resolution of international tensions. Rooted in the five principles of peaceful coexistence (*Panchsheel*), the movement stands for an alternative to confrontation.

12

13

14

15

16

8 Vijaya Lakshmi Pandit, the younger sister of Pandit Jawaharlal Nehru, was the first woman to be elected President of the UN General Assembly (1953–54).

9 UN Flag Series of 1985.

10 Republic of Korea was the first foreign country to bring out stamps depicting the Indian national flag in 1951 to express gratitude to the war-participating countries.

11 Stamp issued in 1965 on the occasion of the 15th anniversary of the Korean War.

12 50th Anniversary of Bandung Conference (1955–2005).

13, 14 Left to right: 10th Non-Aligned Summit Conference, Jakarta 1992; 5th Non-Aligned Summit Conference, Colombo 1976.

15 Flags of UNSC member countries–1992.

16 The UN 'Flag and Coin' series–2007.

17

18

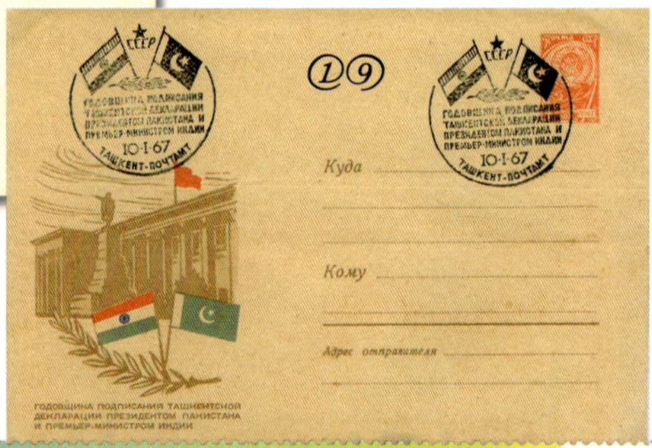

19

20

21

Declaration of international cooperation, solidarities, treaties, etc., between different countries are often expressed and greeted by displaying together the national flags of the countries.

> The Prime Minister of India and the President of Pakistan, having met at Tashkent [Uzbekistan] and having discussed the existing relations between India and Pakistan hereby declare their firm resolve to restore normal and peaceful relations between their countries and to promote understanding and friendly relations between their peoples. They considered the attainment of these objectives of vital importance for the welfare of the 600 million people of India and Pakistan.[2]

Uses of flags during state visits

Official visits of heads of states and other dignitaries are demonstrated by displaying their respective national flags placed side by side or on a crossed staff.

22

23

②④

Stamps were issued to commemorate the state visit of Dr S. Radhakrishnan, President of India, to Iran, in 1963 (see illustration 24).

A stamp was issued to commemorate the president of South Korea's planned state visit to India in October 1983 (see illustration 25). Unfortunately the visit was abandoned just a day before, following an assassination attempt on the Korean president in Rangoon, Myanmar and the stamp was immediately withdrawn from sale.

The Indian Prime Minister, Manmohan Singh, visited Bhutan in 2008 to commemorate the Indo-Bhutan friendship, the coronation of Bhutan's fifth Druk Gyalpo (king of Bhutan) and centenary celebrations of monarchy.

②⑤

②⑥

①⑦ The Indian national flag is printed upside down on this Greek stamp issued in 1989 to commemorate the fifth anniversary of the 'Delhi Declaration of Six-Nation Initiative—1985' for peace and disarmament. The flags of Tanzania and Mexico are also displayed upside down.

①⑧ Kuwait thanked the countries of the world (including India) for joining an international coalition for the liberation of Kuwait in 1991. Special note: 87x134mm, imperforate stamp.

①⑨ Special postmark from Tashkent, dated 10 January 1967, commemorating the first anniversary of the 'Tashkent Declaration–1966'.

②⓪ Flags of India and Palestine Liberation Organisation (PLO). This stamp was issued on the International Day of Solidarity with the Palestinian People on 29 November 1981.

②① World Peace Day se-tenant stamps from Bosnia-Herzegovina–1997.

②② L.I. Brezhnev's first state visit to India in 1973 as General Secretary of the Communist Party of the Soviet Union (CPSU), Central Committee.

②③ L.I. Brezhnev's second state visit to India in 1980, as General Secretary of the CPSU and President of the USSR.

Role of flags in bilateral cooperation

27

28

29

Bilateral cooperation on important and strategic fields is often demonstrated by flying the national flags together.

Role of flags in diplomatic relations

The use of flags in diplomatic relations provides the larger context of the countries they represent. In a meeting of individuals, they act as signifiers of entire nations.

30

The Commonwealth of Nations

The Commonwealth of Nations, formerly known as the British Commonwealth, constituted as far back as the 1880s, is now an intergovernmental organisation of independent member states. Except for a few, most of the member countries were formerly a part of the British Empire. This association was reconstituted by the London Declaration in 1949, when it was agreed that all countries would be freely and equally associated.

31

32

33

34

35

South Asian Association for Regional Cooperation (SAARC)

The idea of regional cooperation in South Asia was mooted by Bangladesh and concurrence to this idea by the governments of Bangladesh, Bhutan, India, the Maldives, Nepal, Pakistan and Sri Lanka resulted in the birth of SAARC on 8 December 1985.

In order to celebrate the birth of the SAARC, each of the seven member countries issued commemorative stamps on 8 August 1985.

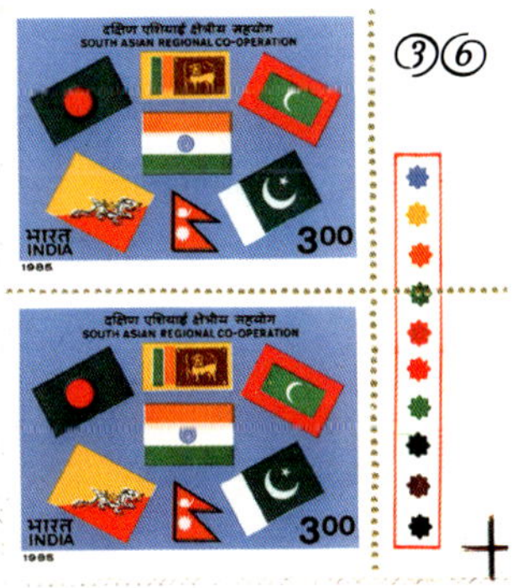

36

37

38

39

40

41

The ceremony for the cancellation of commemorative stamps issued by the seven South Asian countries on the occasion of the launch of the SAARC had to be called off at the last moment. This happened after it was detected that Pakistan's commemorative stamp depicted Jammu and Kashmir as a separate country. This was immediately brought to the notice of the Indian Prime Minister, Rajiv Gandhi, who expressed his objection to it to the Bangladesh president, the

24 National flags of Iran and India respectively.

25 Stamps issued to commemorate president of South Korea's planned (ultimately cancelled) state visit to India in 1983.

26 State visit to Bhutan by Indian Prime Minister, Dr Manmohan Singh.

27 Festival of the USSR in India, 1987.

28 25th anniversary of Indo-Soviet Shipping, 1981.

29 Indo-Soviet cooperation, 1976.

30 The 50th anniversary of diplomatic relations between Bulgaria and India (1954–2004).

31 27th Commonwealth Parliamentary Association Conference 1981. The Indian flag appears on the margin of the miniature sheet.

32 Commonwealth Day, 14 March 1983.

33, 34, 35 Commonwealth Heads of Government Meeting, 1971. Flags of the member countries.

36 SAARC commemorative stamps issued by India.

37 SAARC commemorative stamp issued by Nepal.

chairman of the SAARC. The stamp cancellation ceremony, which was a part of the concluding session of the summit, was then scrapped.

The Pakistani stamp of Re 1 denomination (see illustration 42) showed Jammu and Kashmir as a separate country with a clear demarcating line separating it from India. The controversial Pakistani stamp was withdrawn from sale on 9 August 1985, the very next day.

On similar grounds, the Maldives stamp of Rf. 5 denomination, in which Sikkim had not been shown as a part of India, was withdrawn and so was the Sri Lankan stamp of 60 cents denomination because of the presence of certain anomalies withdrawn the very next day on 9 December 1985.

The philatelic exhibition held on the occasion of the SAARC summit was inaugurated on 7 August in Dhaka, a day before it began. The Indian prime minister, who was scheduled to visit the exhibition, did so only after the controversial stamps were removed from the exhibition.

The SAARC, the world's largest regional grouping, began its 14th summit in New Delhi, on 3 April 2007, where Afghanistan became its eighth member.

42

43

44

45

46

47

48

49

50

51

52

38 SAARC commemorative stamp issued by Maldives.

39, 40 SAARC commemorative stamps issued by Bhutan.

41 SAARC commemorative stamp issued by Bangladesh.

42 SAARC commemorative stamp of Re 1 denomination issued by Pakistan was withdrawn a day after its release due to its controversial demarcation of Jammu and Kashmir as a separate country.

43 SAARC commemorative stamps issued by Sri Lanka. The 60 cents stamp was withdrawn a day after its release due to certain anomalies.

44, 45, 46, 47, 48, 49 Stamps issued by the SAARC member countries from time to time.

50, 51, 52 More stamps issued by SAARC member countries.

Flags and cultural ties

The first contact between the Indian and Greek civilisations dates back to Alexander the Great's conquest in India. For several centuries Indo-Greek kingdoms ruled Gandhara and parts of north-west India.

The island of Jersey takes pride in being a multicultural nation. The Jersey stamps issued in 2006 show Indian national costumes against the backdrop of the Indian national flag (see illustration 56).

53

56

54

55

57

58

59

60

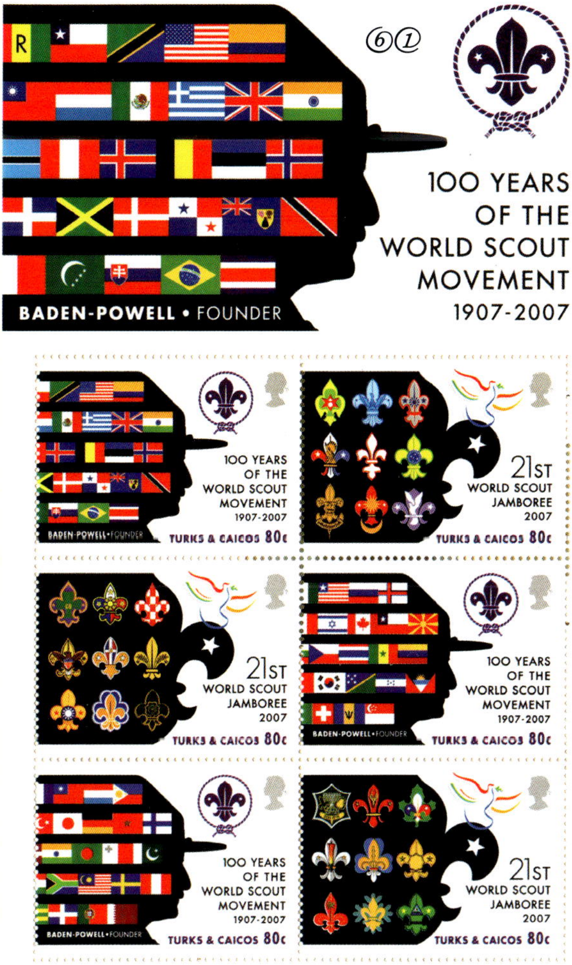

⑥①

⑥②

⑤③ *'Greeks Abroad.' Stamp issued in 1977 to honour Greek expatriates residing around the world, including India.*

⑤④ *The 7th Summit level of the 'Group of 15'. Kuala Lumpur, 1997.*

⑤⑤ *International Literacy Symposium, Teheran, 1975: flags of the participating nations.*

⑤⑥ *Stamps issued by Jersey to celebrate its multicultural spirit.*

⑤⑦ *75th anniversary of Rotary International–1980.*

⑤⑧ *'Rehabilitation in India'. The Salvation Army World Service, 1988.*

⑤⑨ *The postmark of Asian Indians in North America has the Indian national flag on its logo.*

⑥⓪ *The national anthems of Bangladesh and India were written by Nobel laureate Rabindranath Tagore. The miniature sheet was issued by Bangladesh on the occasion of the joint celebration of Tagore's 150th birth anniversary on 6 May 2011.*

⑥①, ⑥② *Stamps issued on the occasion of 100 years of World Scout Movement (1907–2007).*

Flags in Olympic Games

The Olympic flag was designed by Baron Pierre de Coubertin of France, reviver of the Olympic Games in the modern era in 1913. It is a white flag with five interlaced rings in the centre representing the five continents joined in the Olympic movement. The rings are blue, yellow, black, green and red, with the blue ring displayed high on the side nearest to the flagpole. At least one of the colours of the rings appears in the national flag of every country in the world.

63

64

The Olympic flag was raised for the first time in the 'Games of the VII Olympiad' in Antwerp, Belgium in 1920. Coincidentally, India participated with an official team in the Summer Olympiad at Antwerp for the first time.

65

During ongoing Games, both in the stadium and in its surrounding areas, the Olympic flag is flown freely along with the flags of the participating nations. At the opening and closing ceremonies of the Games, there is a parade of athletes: each contingent, dressed in its official uniform, must be preceded by a shield bearing the name of the country, accompanied by its national flag. It is a huge honour for any athlete who is selected to be the 'flag bearer' of his or her country.

66

The Indian flag at international sports events

Nowadays most international sports organisers follow the traditions and practices set forth by the Olympic flag etiquettes.

67

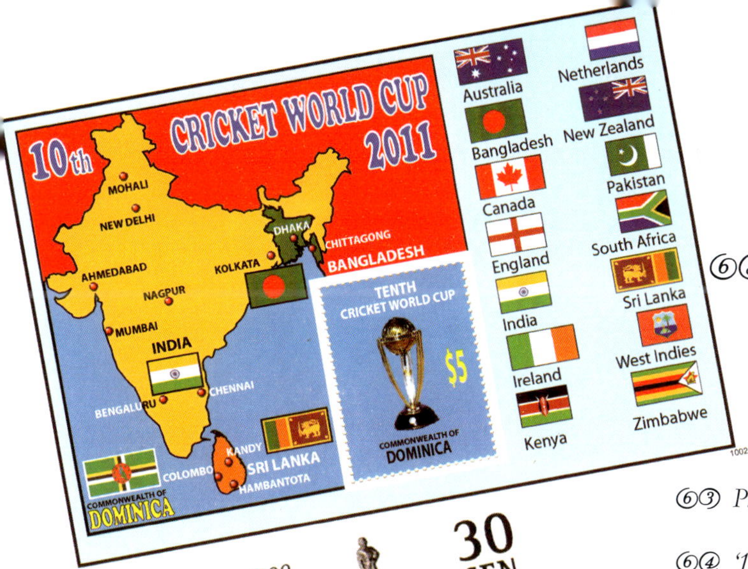

68

69

70

71

72

The ICC World Cup 2011 championship matches were played in India, Bangladesh and Sri Lanka. India won the tournament (see illustration 68).

63 Pierre de Coubertin.

64 '100 years of modern Olympic Games', from Athens 1896 to Atlanta 1996.

65 Olympic winners and the national flag. Scene of India–Pakistan final match, Melbourne, 1956 Olympics.

66 Stamp and postmark commemorating XVII Olympic Winter Games held at Lillehammer, Norway. India failed to qualify in this Olympiad but the flag appears on the stamp.

67 World Cup Hockey Championship 1982 was held in Bombay, India. Depicted on the stamps are flags of the countries that qualified in the tournament.

68 10th Cricket World Cup 2011. Flags of the participating nations appear on the miniature sheet issued by Dominica.

69 Thomas Cup Championship, Malaysia 2000.

70 Third SAF Championship, Dhaka 2003.

The Indian flag displayed during philatelic exhibitions

⑦③

⑦④

⑦⑤

⑦⑥

⑦①, ⑦② Fifth SAF Games, Colombo 1991.

⑦③ World Philatelic Exhibition, Korea 1984.

⑦④ Stamp issued by Sri Lanka to mark a decade of SAARC (1985–1995); postmark of SAARC Philatelic exhibition, Colombo, 1996.

⑦⑤ Indian flag on a stamp issued by Vietnam.

⑦⑥ Stamp issued by Nepal commemorating SAARC Charter Day, 2002; postmark of Nepal Bharat Philatelic Exhibition, 2004.

Endnotes:

1. Whitney Smith, introduction to *Guide to the Flags of the World,* by Mauro Talocci (London: Sidgwick & Jackson, 1982), p. 8.
2. Excerpt from the text of the Tashkent Declaration signed on 10 January 1966, courtesy Government of India Publications.

Flags at Sea

The use of flags at sea was the initiation of flags as they are known today. Flags were made to be actually flown from ship-masts and staffs. At sea etiquettes of how flags should be used and where they should be hoisted and the occasions when they are to be used were formed. Ensign (derived from Greek *semion*, Latin equivalent of *signum*) is the national flag of a ship normally flown at or near the stern.

Indian Navy's White Ensign

Upon becoming a Republic on 26 January 1950, the Indian Navy modified the British White Ensign bearing the Red Cross of St George by replacing the Union Jack with the Indian national flag at the canton.

①

②

③

On 15 August 2001, the Indian Navy dropped the Red Cross of St. George, considered to be a symbol of the patron saint of England, thus smacking of colonial legacy, and adopted a new 'White and Blue' war ensign emblazoned with the naval crest on the fly.

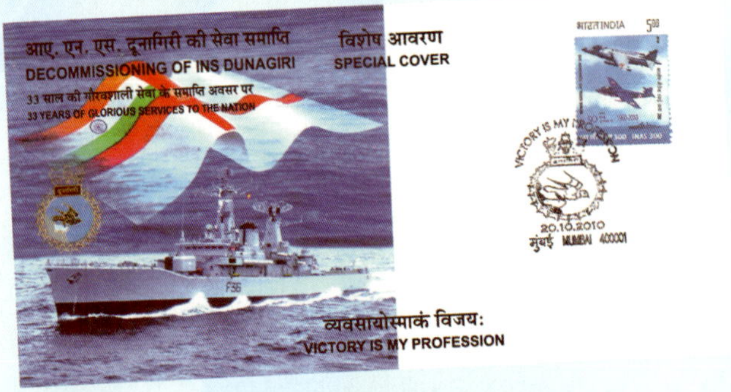

④

The Indian Navy on 25 April 2004, decided to go back somewhat to the original version but now with a vertical and a horizontal red stripe on a white field having the national flag at the canton. The Asoka pillar emblem in golden yellow is now superimposed on the intersection of the red stripes. The new ensign was introduced by the then President and Supreme Commander of the Armed Forces, Dr A.P.J. Abdul Kalam. The day coincided with the return of *INS Tarangini* to her home port at Kochi after going around the world, the first such voyage undertaken by the Indian Navy.

At sea the naval ensign is flown throughout the day and night. During action and combat mission, a warship flies two additional naval ensigns, known as battle ensigns, continuously in conspicuous positions.

⑤

In India the presentation of the President's Colours to a fighting unit carry the highest honour for that unit. It is presented in recognition of the fortitude, resolve and chivalry that a fighting unit displayed in war and in times of stress.

⑥

Indian Blue Ensign

All ships on government duty fly the Blue Ensign defaced by their respective organisation's crest or emblem at the fly, such as the Indian Coast Guard, Port Trusts, River Police, etc.

⑦

The Indian Coast Guard adopted a Blue Ensign defaced by the crest of the Coast Guard at the fly of the flag in 1967 (see illustration 7).

Indian Red Ensign

Indian merchant ships fly the Indian Red Ensign without any defacement or modification whatsoever as the appropriate national colours for Indian ships. Indian ship means a ship registered as such under the Indian Merchant Shipping Act, 1958.

House Flags

Most merchant ships fly a house flag in addition to the Indian Red Ensign. A house flag is usually flown from the ship's masthead.

SS Loyalty of the Scindia Steam Navigation Company, the first Indian ship, wearing the flag of an Indian shipping line, set sail on a commercial voyage from Bombay to the British Isles on 5 April 1919. Since 1964, the day '5th April' is observed as National Maritime Day in India.

⑧

⑨

①, ② Indian Navy's White Ensign. Note how the Indian national flag has replaced the Union Jack at the canton.

③ White and Blue War Ensign. There is a naval crest on the fly. The Red Cross of St George has disappeared.

④ The new Indian Navy ensign featured on the FDC was introduced by President Dr A.P.J. Abdul Kalam on 25 April 2004.

⑤ President's Review of the Fleet.

⑥ Presentation of Colours by the President to the Southern Naval Command. The cover is personally autographed by the then Indian President Giani Zail Singh.

⑦ Postmark celebrating '30 years of Indian Coast Guard', 2007.

⑧ Narottam Morarjee and SS Loyalty.

⑨ The house flag of the Scindia Steam Navigation Co. has the swastika sign in a white circle in the centre of a blue field.

The Scindia Steam Navigation Co. was established by Narottam Morarjee and his associates, Walchand Hirachand, Lalubhai Samal Das and Kilachand Devchand on 27 March 1919.

The Shipping Corporation of India Ltd. (SCI) house flag, in a proportion of 3:2 in saffron colour with the Asoka Chakra with its twenty-four spokes in the centre in blue within a white circle, is taken from the Indian national flag.

The house flag of the SCI has been used from 1950 onwards when one of the constituent companies, the Eastern Shipping Corp. Ltd. of the SCI Ltd. was incorporated.

The slogan 'Patronise national flag ship by Indian ship' was created in order to discourage shipping by Indian shipowners under a flag of convenience, which goes against India's national interest. The Indian National Shipowners' Association (INSA) is the apex body representing and protecting the interests of ship owners across India.

'Flag of Convenience' denotes registry of a merchant ship under a foreign flag. Merchant ships are registered under 'flags of convenience' to reduce

operating costs or to avoid the regulations of their owners' country of origin. Ships registered in a 'flag of convenience' country enjoy nominal registration fees, liberal tax concession, flexibility of investment, no compulsion to employ nationals of the 'flag country' and many such privileges. The International Transport Workers' Federation (ITWF) trusts there should be a 'genuine link' between the real owner of a ship and the flag the ship flies, in accordance with the United Nations Convention on the Law of the Sea (UNCLOS).

①⓪ *Stamp honouring Walchand Hirachand defaced with National Maritime Day special postmark depicting* SS Loyalty.

①① *The Shipping Corporation of India Ltd. (SCI) house flag.*

①② *The franking meter of the Indian National Shipowners' Association (INSA) has the following caption: 'Patronise national flag ship by Indian ship.'*

Military Flags

Since ancient times, warriors carried flags in the battlefield. At first these battle flags were of one colour like all other ancient flags. Gradually, these flags were differentiated by placing inanimate or animate figures on the military flags. Initially, military flags had two purposes—to distinguish between the two forces at war and to mark the position of the leader or the king in battle and thus providing rallying points during confused fighting.

①

②

Regimental or battalion flags are no longer carried during wars in the modern era as a general rule and their uses are mostly restricted to ceremonial purposes.

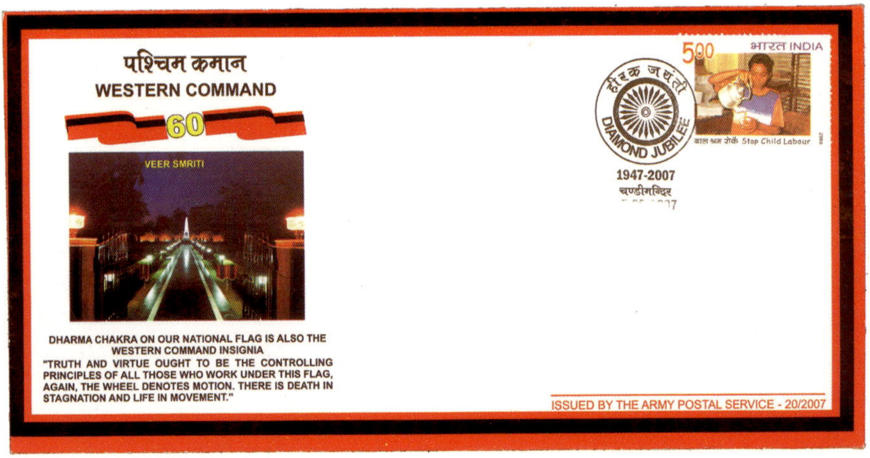

③

④

⑤

The Indian Armed Forces have an elaborate system of ceremonials relating to flags.

At Wagah border (near Amritsar), on the line dividing India and Pakistan, a gate closing ceremony is performed each day about thirty minutes before sunset that ends with a highly stylised 'Retreat Ceremony' called 'lowering of the flags' by the Border Security Force (BSF) of India and Pakistan Rangers. This is a perfectly coordinated ritual that the security forces of India and Pakistan have followed since 1959. At first glance it may appear aggressive and even hostile because the soldiers hurt their feet and knees performing the goose-stepping.

In July 2010, as part of a move initiated by India, both countries agreed to tone down the aggression exhibited by soldiers. Troops of

① Ceremonial flags raised on the occasion of Vijay Divas, 1996.

② Mahar regimental flag on stamp and postmark depicting insignia of Mahar regiment.

③ Dharma Chakra – Western Command insignia special cover issued by the APS.

④ Postmark commemorating Kargil Vijay Divas, 2000, while the envelope bears the photograph of victorious Indian soldiers proudly holding the national flag during the Kargil war.

⑤ 'Flag Day' is the day when funds are raised by sale of small paper (lapel) flags, for the benefit of ex-servicemen. In India, 7 December is observed as Army Flag Day.

⑥

each country pick some of their tallest soldiers – in starched ceremonial uniforms, the Pakistan Rangers in grey salwar-kameezes and the Indian BSFs in khakis with their one-foot-high fan-shaped turbans appearing like crests – to march furiously towards the line separating them. When it seems that they will almost collide together, the guards change direction with a brusque handshake between the soldiers from either side. Then the national flags are slowly lowered in a synchronised move, and the immense metal gates are slammed shut.

⑥ *Retreat Ceremony special cover, issued on 10 January 2012.*

Legal Aspects, Etiquettes and Protocols

The Indian national flag is the symbol of India's national pride, its freedom and sovereignty. There is universal affection and respect for the national flag. After more than five decades of independence and a few years of legal battles, the Government of India lifted the ban on the use of the flag by ordinary citizens on all days in 2002. In terms of the amended and liberalised 'Flag Code of India', 2002, promulgated by the Ministry of Home Affairs, Government of India, there is no restriction on the display of the national flag by the members of the general public, private organisations and educational institutions, etc., except to the extent provided in the Emblems and Names (Prevention of Improper Use) Act, 1950 and the Prevention of Insults to National Honour Act, 1971 and any other law enacted on the subject.

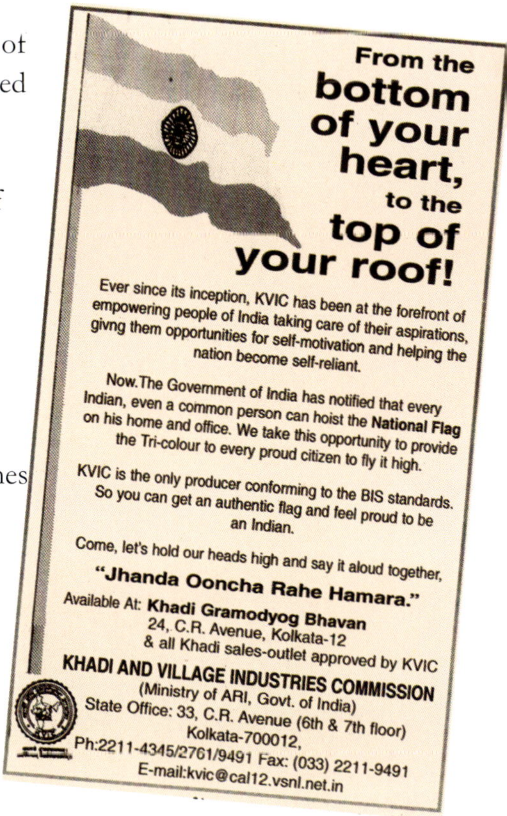

① *Khadi and Village Industries Commission is India's lone national flag producer in nine different sizes conforming to the specifications set by the BIS.*

Keeping in view the provisions of the aforementioned acts, wherever the flag is displayed, it should always occupy the position of honour and be distinctly placed. One way of showing respect to the national flag is to reproduce the flag correctly. On all occasions for official display, only the flags of appropriate sizes conforming to specifications laid down by the Bureau of Indian Standards (BIS) and bearing their standard marks are used. IS 1: 1968 Specification for the national flag of India (cotton khadi), prescribes the design, constructional details and other particulars of the national flag of India. The Standard was originally published in 1951 by the Indian Standards Institution (ISI). The colours of the flag, that is, India saffron (*kesari*), India green and navy blue, shall correspond to the colours in the sealed standard flag held in the custody of the Chief Inspector, Chief Inspectorate of Textiles & Clothing, Kanpur. Variations in shades of a colour should be avoided as these are not generally discernible when a flag is flying. Spectrophotometric values of the white, India saffron and India green colours in the flag presented to the Constituent Assembly on 22 July 1947 were measured by the then Technical Development Establishment Laboratory (Stores), Kanpur. It is intended that the flags made to conform to BIS standards, should have colours as similar as possible to the sealed standard flag. For the purpose of controlling production, sample pieces of bunting dyed with the standard colours may be obtained from the BIS.

②

③

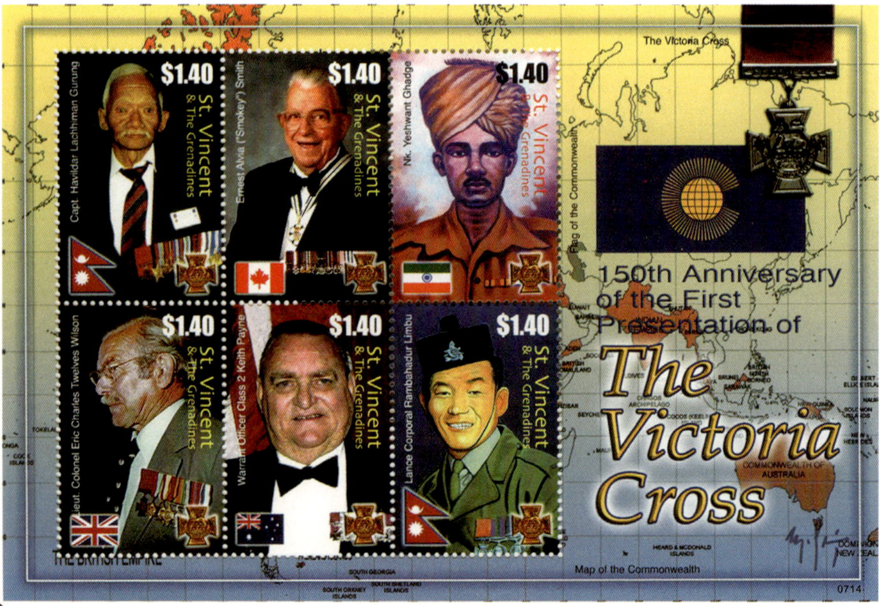

④

Embarrassing situations may occur if outdated or erroneously depicted flags are displayed. The most serious and potentially diplomatically damaging error occurs when a country's flag is incorrectly hoisted. It is important that the national flag is flown the right side up; there is no greater insult than flying a national flag upside down since it shows sheer ignorance and lack of respect.

National Flag in mourning

The association of flags in funerals began centuries ago when caskets of royalty were decorated with their symbols of authority. At times of mourning flags are draped over the coffins of national heroes and other dignitaries. There are specific rules to be observed for draping caskets during a funeral. According to the Flag Code of India, 2002, 'on occasions of State/Military/ Central Paramilitary Forces funerals, the national flag is draped over the bier or coffin with the saffron towards the head of the bier or coffin. The pall flag must be removed from the coffin before it is lowered into the grave or burnt in the pyre.'

The origin of the custom of a flag at 'half-mast' to indicate mourning is yet to be established. But its observance appears to date back to the sixteenth century, as a custom of the sea, which has spread to the land and became universal. Some believe that the flag of mourning is flown at half-mast to leave space for death's invisible flag to be flown above it. The term half-masting is a misnomer as the flag is not flown literally midway between the top and the bottom of the flagstaff, but at a distance down from the tuckhead equivalent to the measurement of the breadth of the flag normally flown. To achieve this position the flag should be first hoisted to the peak for an instant and then slowly lowered to the half-mast position. It should be raised again to the peak before it is lowered for

② Erroneous depiction of the Asoka Chakra with 'twelve spokes' instead of the stipulated 'twenty-four spokes' of the Chakra.

③ Flags of India, Tanzania and Mexico displayed upside down on this Greek stamp issued on 22 May 1989.

④ St. Vincent and the Grenadines inadvertently placed the Indian flag upside down on the stamp issued in honour of Naik Yeshwant Ghagde, recipient of the prestigious Victoria Cross Medal.

⑤ The last journey of Mahatma Gandhi draped in the Indian national flag on a gun carriage.

⑥ Gandhi lying in state, the rising phoenix signifying the continuation of his legacy by Martin Luther King, Jr. (issued in 1992).

⑤

⑥

⑦

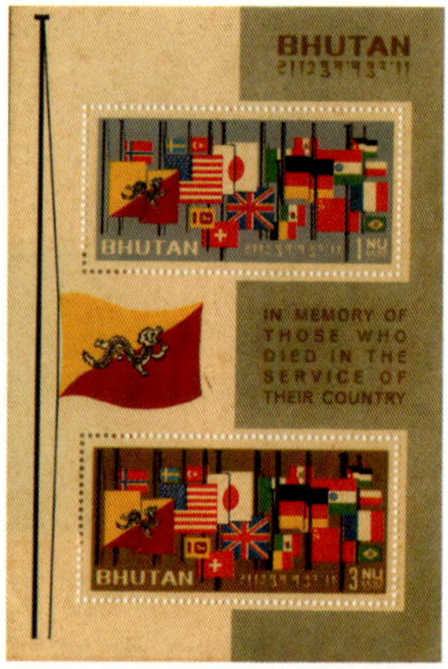

⑧

the day. A further sign of mourning is to attach black ribbons tied as a bow to the top of the flag. The Flag Code stipulates,

> If mourning were to be observed in a parade or procession, where a flag is carried, two streamers of black crepe shall be attached to the spearhead, allowing the streamers to fall naturally. The use of black crepe in such a manner shall only be by an order of the government.

The Flag Code further enumerates,

> Notwithstanding the above provisions, in the event of a 'half-mast day' coinciding with the Republic Day, Independence Day, Mahatma Gandhi's Birthday, National Week (6 to 13 April, in memory of Jalianwala Bagh), any other particular day of National rejoicing as may be specified by the Government, the Flags shall not be flown at half-mast except over the building where the body of the deceased is lying until such time it has been removed and that Flag is raised to the full-mast position after the body has been removed.

⑨

Flying more than one flag

The Flag Code stipulates that when two or more national flags are flown alongside or near each other, then not only should they be at a similar height but of the same superficial area. The flag-masts shall also be of equal size. 'International usage forbids the display of the flag of one nation above that of another nation in time of peace.' The national flag is not to be flown from a single mast-head simultaneously with any other flag or flags. There shall be separate mast-heads for different flags. The general practice is to fly the national flag from the most honourable position, that is, the extreme right with reference to the direction it is facing. Flags of foreign countries, where all are of equal status, shall proceed as from the Indian flag in English alphabetical order. The Indian national flag must be hoisted first and subsequently lowered last.

However, when the United Nation's flag is flown along with the Indian or any other national flags, it can be displayed on either side of the flags. The flag of the UN is flown all over the world on 24 October which is the United Nations Day, and in times of conflict by the UN Forces and Observers. But no national flag flown in its vicinity could be in a higher position or have a larger superficial area.

Display of flags over public buildings

As a rule, the Indian national flag is flown on important public buildings. The flag is flown from sunrise to sunset irrespective of weather conditions. The flag may also be flown on important buildings at night subject to the condition that the flagpole is really tall and the flag is kept well illuminated. The Flag Code states that, 'In frontier areas, the national flag may be flown

10

11

12

13

7 Mother Teresa was given a state funeral to honour her services to the poor and needy in India.

8 National flags are flown at half-mast only by state order.

9 25th anniversary of Indian Independence, a day of national rejoicing, when the national flag shall not be flown at half-mast.

10, 11, 12 The display of the Indian national flag with flags of other nations.

13 UN flag with flags of other nations.

⑭

⑮

⑭, ⑮ Indian flags atop postal heritage buildings: Udagamandalam H.P.O; Delhi G.P.O.

⑯ The Indian national flag displayed on a car on a stamp commemorating 'Special Protection Group'.

on the border customs post, check posts and at other special places where flying of the flag has special significance.'

Display of flags on motor cars

When the national flag is displayed by itself on a motor car, it is flown from a staff, which is fastened either on the middle front of the bonnet or to the right side of the car. The privilege of flying the national flag on motor cars is granted only to a limited number of dignitaries as stipulated in the Flag Code. It further states, 'When a foreign dignitary travels in a car provided by the Indian Government, the Indian national flag is flown on the right side of the car and the flag of the foreign country is flown on the left side of the car.'

⑯

Patriotic Songs: Legacy of the Flag Continues

Patriotic songs are musical equivalents of a country's motto and aspirations. In the words of Joel Barlow (1754–1812), an American revolutionary war songwriter, 'One good song is worth a dozen addresses and proclamations.' Patriotic songs are audible symbols, just as the tricolour flag or the three-faced lion of the Asoka pillar is India's visible national symbol. Many patriotic songs composed at different times and in different Indian languages have references to the flag. Such songs emphasised patriotic sentiments and helped in uniting the people in their common hopes and aspirations.

The stirring song '*Thayin manikodi pareer*' (Behold our Mother's great banner) written by Subramania Bharathiyar (1882–1921) was very popular amongst Tamil-speaking people in India.

Kambathin keelnitral kaneer—engum
Kanarum veerer perunthiru kuttam
Nambar kuriyarav veerer—thangal
Nalluyi ranthunk kodiyinai kapper
Thayin manikodi pareer!

①

(Behold our Mother's great banner!
Under the flag-mast are patriots.
Loyal and faithful
Ready to sacrifice their very life
To keep the flag flying high.
Behold our Mother's great banner!)

'*Jhanda ooncha rahe hamara*' (May our flag always fly high) penned by Shyam Lal Gupt 'Parshad' aroused more patriotic fervour than any other battle cry. The soul-stirring song was first sung on 13 April 1924, at Phoolbag,

②

Kanpur, in remembrance of the Jallianwala Bagh massacre of 1919.

③

Vijayi bishwa tiranga pyara
Jhanda ooncha rahe hamara ...

(World-conquering tricolour dear to us,
May our flag always fly high)

In 1923, Gulab Singh Lodhi was shot dead by the police while unfurling the *Swaraj* flag at Lucknow's Aminudulla park. The park was renamed Jhandewala Park after the incident. *Jhandewala* means 'standard bearer'. The park became the epicentre of political activities in the city of Lucknow. There is a memorial of the '*Jhanda Gaan*' (song of the flag):

④

Jhanda ooncha rahe hamara ...
Sada shakti barsane wala ...
Iski shan na jane paaye ...

(May our flag always fly high …
Constant source of undying strength …
May its glory never fade …)

A patriotic matchbox label (see illustration 5) depicts the *Purna Swaraj* flag with the caption:

⑤

Hamara azadi ka jhanda
Iski izzat hame janse zyada pyari hai.

(The flag of our freedom
Its honour is dearer to us than our lives.)

Subhas Chandra Bose made it his declared intention to raise the 'flag of freedom' atop Delhi's Red Fort. His slogans of '*Jai Hind*' (Victory to India) and '*Chalo Dilli*' (Onward to Delhi) have been immortalised in many post-independence Indian postage stamps.

Sabse ooncha hai duniame
Jhanda hamara
Netaji zindabad ...
Azad karenge, azad karenge
Chalo bhai Dilli chalo
Jhanda laherake chalo ...

(Our flag flies the highest in the whole world
Netaji zindabad ...
We will take our freedom, we will take our freedom
Comrades to Dilli
March with the flag)

The songs of the Indian National Army (INA) captured the hope harboured in every Indian mind—that the 'flag of freedom' will soon be hoisted in Delhi's Red Fort, ushering in India's independence.

① *Special postmark dated 17 December 1982, issued from Anna Road Head Post Office, Chennai, to mark the valedictory day of the birth centenary celebrations of the poet Bharathiyar.*

② *FDC commemorating Shyam Lal Gupt. The postmark features the national flag.*

③ *Paying 'Homage to Martyrs' on the occasion of the 25th anniversary of Independence.*

④ *On one side of the matchbox appears a picture of Subhas Chandra Bose and the pledge to give complete support to the leader.*

⑤ *The* Purna Swaraj *flag and patriotic motto inscribed on the other side of the same matchbox depicted in illustration 4.*

⑥ 'Jai Hind' *and* 'Chalo Dilli' *inscribed on the stamp in Hindi.*

Our national flag's legacy

Tomar pataka jare dao
Tare dao bahibare sakati

(Give strength to the bearer of your flag)
—Rabindranath Tagore

The Children's Day stamp of 1962 carries the theme of the year as conveyed by the International Union for Child Welfare, Geneva: 'The rights of every child; the responsibility of every adult and community.'

Let us repeat together with folded hands the words inscribed in the Flag Code of India, 2002, for the edification of school children, 'I pledge allegiance to the National Flag and to the Sovereign Socialist Secular Democratic Republic for which it stands.'

⑦ 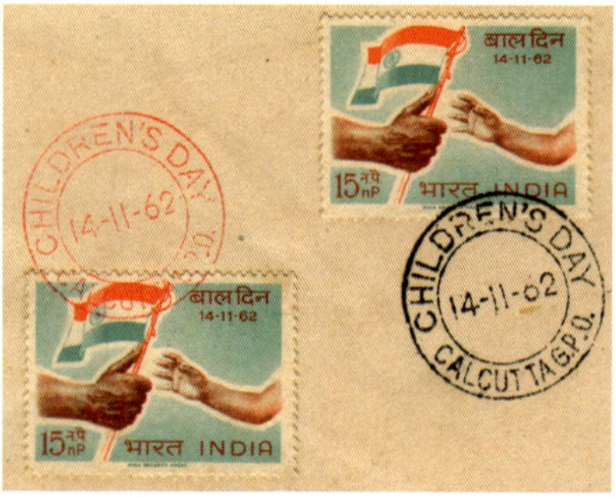

The development of the historic consciousness of the youth of the country depends upon an understanding of the imperatives and the deeply-felt beliefs that informed the creation of the national flag. A concerted attempt will have to be made to educate the generations to come if they are to see the history, the cherished principles and the significance of its very appearance when they see their national flag.

⑦ Stamps depicting the national flag being handed over to the youth, issued to mark Children's Day on 14 November 1962.

The Indian National Flag unfurled through Philately

Appendix-I

'The *Vajra* as a National Flag'
R. S.

The question of the invention of a flag for India is beginning to be discussed in the press. Those who contemplate the desirability of such a symbol, however, seem to be unaware that already a great many people have taken up, and are using, the ancient Indian *Vajra* or Thunderbolt, in this way. When we look at all that a national banner means, we see the utter impossibility of manufacturing or devising such an emblem. It can only grow up out of the heart and history of a people. A trade-mark, a custom-house seal, or a signalling pennant, may be arranged, imposed, prescribed, but a BANNER, with its menace and its rallying-cry, a BANNER, with its benison and call to sacrifice, must be born within the soul of the nation, and call up a passion that none outside the Guardian-race can understand. For this reason, it seems worth while to recapitulate briefly the history and significance of the *Vajra* as an emblem of nationality. For while this symbolism cannot be imparted piecemeal to those outside the circle of its enthusiasm, it can and must be handed on from generation to generation, and province to province. In matters of worship, the mystic lore can only be analysed and explained to those who are already being initiated and to them, must be; so also here we dare not leave our tradition in any half-light of uncertainty, lest our children should grow up in vagueness as to the sign of their unity and common honour.

Throughout the period before the Christian Era, the Thunderbolt as a symbol, was of cosmopolitan importance. Amongst Greeks and Romans, the Eagle of Zeus carried it in his claws. For the Romans, it was a military sign, and a device in perpetual use. It was one of the favourite designs stamped on the little earthen lamps that the housewife brought home from the bazaar. Another was the locust; both evidently symbolising the destructive power of fire. Zeus amongst the Greeks, and Jupiter amongst the Romans, was the wielder of the Thunderbolt. And similarly in India, amongst the Aryan races, Indra was the God of the Thunderbolt. It was natural enough that this should be so. Tidal waves, earthquakes, volcanic eruptions, waterspouts, floods, are all forms of violence that act from below. Only rain and lightning come from above, and of the two lightning is hurled from the remoter height, mysterious, momentary, of a deadly definiteness and certainty of aim, in good sooth the sword of the sky. Farther, to be accounted for on no other terms. Dangerous and wrapped in terror as is the earthquake, it cannot be compared with the thunderbolt in distinctness of form, and in poetry, or, above either of these qualities, in discriminativeness of action. Obviously, to ages whose divinities were at bottom personifications of the forces of nature, it was inevitable that Power Almighty, Cosmic, Infinite, should appear armed with the one weapon of heavenly destructiveness—the thunderbolt. Jupiter, Zeus, and Indra, armed with the *Vajra,* speak for themselves of the past antiquity of the conception, coming, as it does, out of an age when the civilisation of man was one, and continents had not yet attained ethnological distinctness.

The habits of thought of these pre-Buddhistic ages are revealed to us in the sculptures and bas-reliefs of the Buddhist period itself. Again, the characteristic ideas of the Buddhistic centuries find expression in the beginning of the Mahabharata. A new era always opens with a re-statement in some form or other of the convictions of the old. Hence, as Grunwedel points out, in the early delineations of Buddha, Indra is always seen as His supreme worshipper, with the thunderbolt in his hand.

We have here an instance of the way in which the Indian genius renders dynamic and spiritual what would remain in the hands of other races merely static and material. Already, two hundred and fifty years before the crowning of the first Roman Emperor, the Indian people are dreaming of One without miraculous manifestation of any sort, yet so great within that to Him the highest powers of nature are to be subordinate. All things - even the gods - are put under His feet. Yet He is only the man who has attained. We cannot wonder that the Thunderbolt becomes the symbol of Buddha. In the sculptures of our period - after the formation of the *Kutil* script - we find it borne on a sort of shield, at the foot of the panel. Again, it becomes specially identified with one of the Bodhisattvas, and he is known as Vajrapani, a great power, yet to be incarnated, armed with the thunderbolt. In Thibet and in Burma, the thunderbolt stands for Buddha Himself, a fact that one finds abundantly illustrated at Bodh Gaya. The Thibetan Lama does his *puja,* holding a miniature *Vajra* in the left hand. Above all, the famous diamond-throne of the Buddhist world is found, at the same shrine, to be a circular stone, deeply engraved with a circle of *Vajras* and ornamental designs, and known as the *Vajra-Asana*, or Thunderbolt Seat.

Do we desire to fill in the hiatus here, to understand the innermost significance of this identification? Why was Buddha the Thunderbolt? To this question the Mahabharata as we now have it, gives us the answer. At the opening of the Mahabharata, it would be impossible to exaggerate the importance attributed to the Thunderbolt. "Wherever there is glory, or honour, or purity, great wisdom, or great sanctity, or great energy, know that to be a fragment of the Thunderbolt". But the *secret* of this is a different matter. The gods, it is said, were looking for a divine weapon, *par excellence*— and they were told that only if they could find a man willing to give his own bones for the substance of it, could the Invincible Sword be forged. Whereupon they trooped up to the *rishi* Dadhichi and asked for his bones for the purpose. The request sounded like mockery. A man would give all but his own life-breath, assuredly, for a great end, but who, even to furnish forth a weapon for Indra, would hand over his body itself? To the *rishi* Dadhichi, however, this was no insuperable height of sacrifice. Smilingly he listened, smilingly he answered, and in that very moment laid himself down to die - yielding at a word the very utmost demanded of humanity.

Here, then, we have the significance of the *Vajra.* THE SELFLESS MAN IS THE THUNDERBOLT. Let us strive only for selflessness, and we become the weapon in the hands of the gods. Not for us to ask how. Not for us to plan methods. For us, it is only to lay ourselves down at the altar-foot. The gods do the rest. The divine carries us. It is not the thunderbolt that is invincible, but the hand that hurls it. Mother!Mother ! Take away from us this self ! Let not fame or gain or pleasure have dominion over us ! Be Thou the sunlight, we the dew dissolving in its heat.

The Thunderbolt did not cease to have a history, with the closing of the Buddhist period. In India, it probably gave birth to the *trisul* of Siva, and it remains to this day the weapon placed in the lowest of the right hands of Durga, in the autumn *puja.* In Europe, it is quite possible that, through Byzantium, it has determined the form of the sovereign crown. But undoubtedly as a weapon it has grown less dynamic in form, with the progress of time. Nothing could better show the superiority of the Indian mind in decorative instinct, than a comparison of the classical thunderbolt of Europe with that of India. The Roman thunderbolt is a specimen of crude realism; the Indian from the beginning, is graceful and replete with poetry. In its Bodh-Gaya form, as it appears on the *Vajra-Asana*, the meaning has become clear-'the spear concealed in the flower of the lightning.' It is this wonderful phonetic quality that gives the symbol its peculiar appropriateness for a national flag. For above all things, a banner must have phonetic power. Whole nations are proud to be its bodyguard. Instinctively must they translate its crimson into struggle for it, its gold into promised victory, its white into the purity and passion of their own love for land and race. "Red as our love for thee, green as our hope for thee, white as our faith in thee!" sang Swinburne, to the Italian Flag, with its red, white, and green. But meanings like these cannot be learnt. They must spring up spontaneously, self-prompted by the first glance at the waving scarf, the first grip of the hand upon its staff. The eagles of Rome, or of Napoleon, the *fleur-de-lys* of mediaeval France, the stars and stripes of the American States, - what a spell these cast, by their very names, upon the hearts of men! This is the secret appeal of the standard to its chosen souls. This is the call that stirs their blood to the madness of devotion, the spiritual *reveille* – Awake !Awake ! – that could not be resisted if we would, that must be followed, whenever and wherever it may lead.

But the future is never exactly as the past. And the new symbol cannot be even as the old. Hence the Thunderbolt of present day use is crossed. That is to say, it is multiplied in power, as befits the aspiration that is not of a great man here and there, but of every soul in a vast nation, at the same time. It is India, in all her millions, not a few Indian saints or prophets, who is called today to attain selflessness. India in the might of her brotherhood. India in her unity, India in the cohesion of a single body, has to go down, down, down, into the depths, in order to climb the mountains of perfect strength and gaze upon the Promised Land.

It is for this that the Thunderbolt is multiplied, that it may be the symbol, not of a hero, but of a nation of heroes. With the same idea, also, of expressing in the national emblem the unity of India, many people use the lotus for the reverse of the flag. Very few probably know the beautiful old map of Varaha-Mihira (about A.D. 550) in which India is represented as an eight-petalled lotus, where Panchala is the centre, and Magadha, Kalinga, Avanta, Amarta, Sindhu, Harhama, Madra, and Kulinda form the eight petals. India as the lotus, the lotus lying on the Ocean, or India as Uma practising austerities to be the bride of Mahadeva, - it is difficult, sometimes, to believe that our old poets did not directly and deliberately idealise their country!

When we think of all that a national banner represents, we cannot wonder that the standards were the only things contained in the chapel of the Praetorium, in Roman times. We feel their sacredness, alike in war and peace. We thrill to the thought of the shot-riddled flags brought home from European battle-fields and hung beside the altar, in churches and cathedrals. To a people who understand their own nationality, no other guerdon can be half so precious. For a banner is at once a benison and a menace, a consecration and a rallying-cry. It is as an altar, at whose foot, whether for assault or defence, men's lives are freely offered up. Generations come and go. New combinations arrive and vanish, but that for which the national symbol stands - that ineffable union of *jana-desha-dharma* for which every people fights - remains for ever, simple and steadfast as Eternity, mirrored in the fugitive minds of its myriad worshippers.

(*Modern Review*, November 1909)

Appendix-II

'The National Flag' by M.K. Gandhi

A flag is a necessity for all nations. Millions have died for it, it is no doubt a kind of idolatry which it would be a sin to destroy. For a flag represents an ideal. The unfurling of the Union Jack evokes in the English breast sentiments whose strength it is difficult to measure. The Stars and Stripes mean a world to the Americans. The Star and the Crescent will call forth the best bravery in Islam.

It will be necessary for us Indians-Hindus, Mohammedans, Christians, Jews, Parsis, and all others to whom India is their home-to recognise a common flag to live and to die for.

Mr. P Venkayya of the National College, Masulipatam, has for some years placed before the public a suggestive booklet describing the flags of the other nations and offering designs for an Indian National-Flag. But, whilst I have always admired the persistent zeal with which Mr. Venkayya has prosecuted the cause of a National-Flag at every session of the Congress for the past four years, he was never able to enthuse me; and in his designs I saw nothing to stir the nation to its depths. It was reserved for a Punjabi to make a suggestion that at once arrested attention. It was Lala Hansraj of Jullundur who, in discussing the possibilities of the spinning wheel, suggested that it should find a place on our *Swaraj-Flag*. I could not help admiring the originality of the suggestion. At Bezwada I asked Mr. Venkayya to give me a design containing a spinning wheel on a red (Hindu Colour) and Green (Muslim colour) background. His enthusiastic spirit enabled me to possess a flag in three hours. It was just a little late for presentation to the All-India Congress Committee. I am glad it was so. On maturer consideration I saw that the background should represent the other religions also. Hindu-Muslim unity is not an exclusive term; it is an inclusive term, symbolic of the unity of all faiths domiciled in India. If Hindus and Muslims can tolerate each other, they are together bound to tolerate all other faiths. The unity is not a menace to the other faiths represented in India or to the world. So I suggest that the background should be white and green and red. The white portion is intended to represent all other faiths. The weakest numerically occupy the first place. The Islamic colour comes next; the Hindu colour red comes last, the idea being that the strongest should act as a shield to the weakest. The white colour moreover represents purity and peace. Our National-Flag must mean that or nothing. And to represent the equality of the least of us with the best, an equal part is assigned to all the three colours in the design.

But India as a nation can live and die only for the spinning-wheel. Every woman will tell the curious that with the disappearance of the spinning-wheel, vanished India's happiness and prosperity. The womanhood and the masses of India have been awakened as never before at the call of the spinning-wheel. The masses recognise in it the giver of life. The women regard it as the protector of their chastity. Every widow I have met has recognised in the wheel a dear forgotten friend. Its restoration alone can fill the millions of hungry mouths. No industrial development scheme can solve the problem of the growing poverty of the peasantry of India covering a vast surface 1,900 miles long and 1,500 broad. India is not a small island; it is a big continent, which cannot be converted like England into an industrial country. And we must resolutely set surface against any scheme of exploitation of the world. Our only hope must centre upon utilising the wasted hours of the nation, for adding to the wealth of the country, by converting cotton into cloth in our cottages. The spinning-wheel is, therefore, as much a necessity of Indian life as air and water.

Moreover, the Muslims swear by it just as much as the Hindus. As a matter of fact, the former are taking to it more readily than the Hindus. For the Muslim woman is purdanashin and she can now add a few paisas to the poor resources that her husband brings to the family. The spinning-wheel, therefore, is the most natural, as it is the most important, common factor of national life. Through it we inform the whole world that we are determined, so far as our food and clothing are concerned, to be totally independent of the rest of it. Those who believe with me will make haste to introduce the spinning-wheel in their home and possess a National-Flag of the design suggested by me.

It follows that the flag must be made of *Khaddar*, for it is [through] rough coarse cloth alone that we can make India independent of foreign markets for her cloth. I would advise all religious organisations, if they agree with my argument, to weave into their religious flags, as for instance the Khilafat, a miniature National-Flag in the upper left hand corner. The regulation size of the Flag should contain the drawing of a full sized spinning-wheel.

(First Published in *Young India*, April 1921)

Appendix-III

'The National Flag' by Prof. Suniti Kumar Chatterji

Dedication
To SIR SARVAPALLI RADHAKRISHNAN
Vice-Chancellor, Hindu University, Benares.
Teacher, Thinker, Writer,
Interpreter of India.

As a little token of admiration and affection from his former colleague in the University of Calcutta
The Author

At the last session of the Congress it was decided to go into the question of the National Flag. It was a good thing that this decision was finally arrived at. A flag stands as a symbol of something; and a National Flag is the symbol of our national ideals and aspirations, of our hopes and achievements as a people. It is a beacon light, showing to the people the path to sacrifice, often to the supreme sacrifice; 'they are hanging men upon the common, for the wearing of the green'. Consequently it is not to be treated lightly as something, which need not have any special or deep significance. The Flag Committee of the Congress fortunately realises the importance of the question, and also their responsibility in the matter. Dr. Pattabhi Sitaramayya, the Convener of the Committee, has issued a questionnaire inviting opinions from different Congress and other organisations, as well as from individuals.

~

There is no ancient flag or banner whether of Hindu or Muhammadan times, which we can think of for adoption as the flag of our country as a whole. Imperial or local princely houses had their standards, e.g. the *Garuda* Standard of the Imperial Guptas. But even when nearly the whole of India was united under the Mauryas in the 3rd century B.C. and the Moguls in the 17th century A.C. [sic] no national flag or crest seems to have been thought of. India was never physically a *nation militante*, and so there was no need for a national symbol to rally round, in opposition to other nations. Besides, the *political* unity of India that we are now conscious of is an entirely new thing. But underlying this new sense of political unity is the unseen foundation of a sense of *geographical* and *cultural* unity which is age-old in our history, and which transcends all diversities and oppositions of race, language, and creed.

If we set about trying to find a National Flag for India, what would be, in the first instance, the right attitude to take up? If we aim at having a united Indian nation – or a federation of Indian nationalities – we must not, as the most solemn article of our political creed, countenance anything that will help to perpetuate cleavages in the community. *We must not think in terms of different communities, whatever be their language or religion or geographical situation.* We cannot, therefore, think of quartering our National Flag to perpetuate a sense of communal distinctness among our people. Any explanation of the colours in our National Flag as symbolising Hindus, Musalmans, Christians and other communities we should regard as pernicious and anti-national.

The colours in a national flag for a country like India, which has been the most remarkable meeting-ground of peoples, should thus represent ideas and aspirations which are of universal significance and which have no merely accidental connexion with this or that section's past – a past which is sought to be employed for communal or national chauvinism. If any particular community finds a secret pleasure in thinking of a certain colour or symbol which has been adopted in the National Flag as being specially connected with its own little or big world within the bigger world of India, either spiritually or historically, it does not matter, so long as that is not forced upon the national interpretation and so long as other communities also find it appropriate, from a national, supra-communal stand-point.

Let us now see how far the National Flag in use at present satisfies the above and other considerations.

In the case of the national flag and crest we have, like many national anthems, either an accidental beginning at the psychological moment, or a deliberate promulgation. The official British flag for India (the Union Jack with a star with an English motto "Heaven's Light Our Guide") belonging to the latter category and having no reference to our history and traditions or to anything universal, could have no appeal for the Indian body politic; and the need for a truly Indian flag was felt by our leaders. There were many tentative essays at flag-making; a green field with five white lotuses in a row here, a white lotus in a red field there, an outline map of India on a blue background at some other place. More than twenty years ago the late Sister Nivedita suggested in an article in the *Modern-Review* a design for the National Flag in which the Thunderbolt and the Lotus were included, to symbolise the spiritual aspirations of India. Green and Red were probably first hoisted as the national colours for India by Mrs. Annie Besant and

Mr. Wadia in the year 1917. Green then stood for Life and Hope, and Red for Blood and Sacrifice. In 1921-22 the white was added to the Red and Green, and with the political atmosphere being surcharged with the spirit of Khilafatism and communal compartmentalism, the communal interpretation of the colours came into being – Green was made to represent the Muhammadans, Red the Hindus, and the neutral White all the lesser communities.

Objections were put forward to these colours from time to time, but a general loyalty to Mahatmaji and to the Congress and the intensity of the political struggle did not allow any serious opinion to crystallise. Sanskrit scholars at the All-India Sanskrit Conference held in Calcutta in 1924 mildly talked of including Saffron or Ochre colour and the *Gada* mace of Vishnu as Hindu symbols in the flag. On the eve of the Belgaum session of the Congress in 1924 a letter was sent from Rabindranath's institution at Santiniketan, signed, among others, by the late Dwijendranath Tagore and C.F. Andrews, requesting Mahatmaji to consider the advisability of including the *gairika (geru,* or red ochre colour) in the National Flag. It typified the spirit of renunciation and was a colour, which symbolised an ideal common to the Hindu Yogi and Sannyasi as well as to the Muslim Faqir and Darwesh. (See in this connexion the *Modern Review* for November 1930). Recently the Sikhs brought the question to a head by making a firm demand that the Sikh colour, which is equally the *geru* or saffron, should have a place in the National Flag.

~

Let us see what objections can be urged against the present Red, White and Green National Flag. In the first instance these three colours, and these three only, already figure in the flags of at least four different countries – Persia and Italy, and Bulgaria and Mexico. The dispositions of the colours are different, but Bulgaria has an identical arrangement with the present Indian Flag. We do not know what these three colours symbolise for the peoples of the above countries. But why not let India have something distinctive, something in the way of colour, which one can specially connect with her and her ideals? More-over, the communal symbolism suggested for the colours in our Flag is to be objected to; and further objection can be made for both the Red and the White even on these communal grounds.

We should (at least in the authoritative Congress explanation of the device) expunge all communal connotations, and further substitute some new colour-scheme consisting of three or more colours (cf. China, which has five horizontal bars of red, yellow, blue, white and black). We can retain three, falling in a line with most countries; our tricolour will then be described, in our democratic language, as the *Hindusthan-ka-Tiranga Jhanda.* Or, we can have four colours; we shall then call our flag the *Chauranga,* which by itself, like the French *tricolore,* will suffice to indicate the Indian national Flag. *Four* is a number we are fond of in India. It is the basis of computation in our monetary system, in our weights and measures, and in our game of chess (*Chaturanga* i.e. the four wings of the army, Persianised and Arabicised into *shatranj)*, a great gift of India to the world. So four colours would be quite distinctive of India if included in the Indian Flag.

What should these three colours, or four, be? What should they represent? A symbol, when it once has obtained a vogue, should not be disturbed, for two reasons. It has to be seen whether there is anything really objectionable against a symbol as such: if there is none, then there is no point in trying to improve upon it. Then, we must not disturb a state of things which is crystallising as something very necessary in our national life and consciousness. Now, for the last ten years the present National Flag is being used throughout the length and breadth of this country. And these last ten years have witnessed, under the shadow of this banner, a wonderful transformation of our Indian people. We should not consequently bring in any violent or revolutionary change in our National Flag; we should, if some change is thought necessary, bring in the minimum amount of alteration required under the circumstances.

~

I wish to reiterate once again that a communal explanation or allocation of colours, like communal electorates, should be taboo. We should keep away from this poison as much as possible. We can easily revert to the original explanation of these Colours as Symbols of Ideas – the explanation of which is also universal. I think Green and Red should both be retained. Green, the colour of vegetation, is the colour of life and growth, and this symbolism is current among all the nations of the earth. As a people, above all we want to live, and we can very well have the symbol of Life in our national emblem. Green is also the colour of Hope, and we live largely in hope. As we want to live we want to strive – we want to fulfil a purpose in our existence. Life for us should be something more than mere existence. It is a quest – it is a kind of ardour which would rise superior to all oppositions, material, moral and spiritual, in our realisation of the Ideal.

Life is indeed *Passion,* taking the neutral sense of the word – the passion which throbs in our breast and which tingles in the life-blood in us. Red is the colour of this quality in our life; call it Passion or Suffering, call it Exultation or Triumph, call it Sacrifice that is necessary for both. Red, the colour of blood is the most appropriate colour for this Passion – this *Raga,* and this Sacrifice – which the blood crushed out of the victim's existence enables us to visualise most forcefully. Green and Red, therefore, both are appropriate; they are the symbols of life which is a perpetual striving and sacrifice; not petty symbols of a community or a minority, eagerly jostling with others for a place in the sun.

~

What should the third colour be, if we elect to retain three colours? Should the White, too, be retained? I think here practical considerations in the first instance should make us pause before we can finally accept the White. White is a good colour, it is a universal symbol of Purity. But it is likewise a colour which we associate in India with Mourning. But weightier than this is the fact that White already occurs with Red and Green in the flags of four other countries, as mentioned before. And everywhere White does not connote purity. In the French tricolour, White is retained as the monarchist colour – the colour of the Bourbon house. This practical consideration should make us think of some other better (or at least equally suitable) colour. And it will be an additional point in favour of that colour if we can connect it in a special manner with our country.

~

It seems that the ideas of Renunciation and Harmlessness – of *Vairagya* and *Ahimsa* – form the keynote of Indian life, whether Hindu or Muhammadan or Christian. This is the ideal which would send the king in his old age to the forest hermitage in Hindu India; this same Ideal of Renunciation made Prince Siddhartha, the Buddha that was to be, don the saffron garb of the ascetic; and behind the magnificence of the Mogul court it was this ideal, again, which dominated the eclectic Akbar, whose great principle in life was *Sulh-e-Kull* or 'peace with all', and the austere Aurangzeb whose single-minded devotion to the strait (sic) path enjoined by the faith in which he was born soared up in the firmament of his career with the unbroken flight of a tall mosque minaret. An Indian is never in so great love with life and its possessions as to think highly of a 'death in harness' in his old age; life has far deeper and more mysterious meaning for him than piling up the goods of the world, or going on building something and yet starving his soul. He would rather be a mendicant in the shrine of his own faith and pious contemplation, guiding and helping his followers and yet feeling detached from them. That is why the faith in the unseen world and preparation for it which Islam teaches with such insistence found a congenial soil in India, more than perhaps in any other land where Islam penetrated. The ideal of Harmlessness is also present in the mystic and the deeper expression of Islam that is Sufism. And the Indian always associated with this spirit of detachment and of *Ahimsa* the reddish or orange-brown colour of the garments worn by the wanderer. The *geru* or *gairika,* the Red Ochre or Saffron colour worn by the Indian *Sannyasi* brings to our mind most forcibly the picture of this great ideal of Detachment and Harmlessness. This Saffron colour also is the colour of discipline in life, physically or morally and spiritually, for it is the colour enjoined upon the *Brahmacharin.* A modification of this Saffron colour is the Yellowish Brown – the *Kasava* or *Kashaya* – of Buddhism, where it is the great symbol of the Buddhist brotherhood with its insistence on *Ahimsa.* This colour is of the Earth – it is a kind of *khaki,* for the red ochre is a pigment which is a gift of Mother Earth. This red-brown tint of the earth has also been accepted by Islam in India, for Muhammadan *Faqirs* with robes dyed in *geru* are as much the wanderers over the highways of India as are their brothers in the quest, the Hindu *Sadhus.* It does not require much imagination or sense of the fitness of things to feel that in India's National Flag her great message of *Brahmacharya, Ahimsa* and *Vairagya* should be symbolised by a colour which has been associated by her people with these ideals from time immemorial.

~

Red, Green and Ochre or Saffron would thus be a distinctive colour scheme for India. The cloth for the National Flag should in all cases be hand-spun and hand-woven – whether cotton or silk.

There would then be less chance of confusing our national colours with other nations like Persia and Italy, Mexico and Bulgaria. The disposition of these colours should be vertical rather than horizontal, preferably with Red next to the staff, Ochre or Saffron at the outer edge, and Green in the middle. A vertical arrangement is suggested because the oblong vertical blocks give an idea of robustness and strength which the supine horizontal blocks, one lying above another, fail to do. Any one would be convinced of that by contemplating the pictures of the flags of the different nations side by side.

The idea of having *four* colours may also be considered. In that case, the retention of the neutral White with addition of the Saffron may be advocated. We shall have a representation of the Ideal of Purity as well. Here again the White might figure after the Red for better effect.

~

The colours as representing ideals or sentiments of universal appeal and yet with a special Indian touch in the Ochre or Saffron can be symbols of manifold power and significance, and can have more meanings and more kinds of appeal to communities or individuals within the state. If the Musalman thinks of the great brotherhood of Islam when he contemplates the Green in this Flag, and if he finds pleasure in thinking that his creed with its insistence upon the Unity of Godhead is represented with its traditional colour-symbol in his National Flag, other communities will also rejoice with him and appreciate his special affection for the ideals of the democratic faith of Islam. If the Christian sees in the Red the blood of his Lord, which, by His supreme act of sacrifice, helps to make men cleaner and whiter, we shall be equally happy that such a noble ideal should also be thought to have a place in our national emblem. And if the Hindu, whether Sanatani or Brahmo or Arya-Samaji, or Buddhist or Jain or Sikh, reveres the National Flag with greater awe as containing the symbol of *Vairagya* and *Ahimsa,* every true Musalman and Christian will be equally glad for it. And if four colours are decided upon, and the White is retained, those who love the Ideal of Purity which is present through all faiths – and sometimes transcends them, it may be – will have as citizens of India an equal cause for rejoicing. Thus the Hindus of Bali in Indonesia please themselves by regarding the Red, White and Blue banner of Holland as representing respectively Brahma, Siva and Vishnu; - and the Dutch, too feel pleased at this Balinese interpretation.

~

Should we have any device on the Flag – Red, Green and Ochre, or Red, White, Green and Ochre? Most countries have a device, in addition to the national colours; e.g. Ireland has the Shamrock and the Harp, Mexico the Cactus Plant with an Eagle carrying a Snake, England the Rose, the Soviet Union the Hammer and Sickle, etc. The *Charkha* or Spinning Wheel has been in use with our National Flag, being painted in blue on its body. It represents India's desire for the simple life, and her will to combat poverty with the wholesome remedy of her cottage industries. But the *Khaddar* cloth itself as the product of the *Charkha* amply indicates this ideal. The Spinning

Wheel as a device on a flag is cumbrous. We do not want to have a sword or a thunderbolt, or some plant or animal figure, –that will not be acceptable to all. But simplifying the *Charkha*, we might have a Simple Wheel.

~

A Simple Wheel is the most eloquent of symbols. It represents Eternity; it represents Time; it stands for Progress, it figures the Universe. We can put any great idea or meaning to it, and it will not be vulgar. In Persian, the word for wheel, *charkh,* signifies also the celestial globe, the sphere of the heavens, as well as circular motion and fortune. The ancient Indian use of this symbol is as varied as it is profound. We can have symbol of Eternity as something mystic behind existence as an embellishment of our National Flag. Besides, this symbol can further be employed in a most appropriate manner to indicate one great fact in our national life in a United States of India – our federalism which in principle has been accepted for the future constitution of our country. The wheel can be made to represent our India as a Federal Union; and we can then take the spokes to stand for the constituent members of the Federation – the various Provinces and States. The American National Flag has a similar device – in its flag of stars and stripes the forty-eight white stars in the blue field indicate the forty-eight Members of the Federation of the United States of America. But it is not necessary to make the number of the Members of the Federation and the spokes of the wheel agree. We need not press the comparison too far. The idea of the individual spokes forming the wheel would be enough, and we can have a wheel of the minimum number of spokes – three, or better four – for the flag; for we should remember the question of making the flag, and so avoid complications. If the wheel idea is thought worthy of consideration – a three or four spoked wheel in yellow or black – either of the colours will go best with the Red and Green – can be suggested, to find a place in the central field of the flag.

It has been suggested by some that it will be appropriate to have a spread-out Lotus, in White, with four or eight petals in place of the Wheel. The Lotus will be certainly poetic, and no one can take exception to this great Symbol of India. But would it not be a little too weak, when compared with the Wheel? Then, a Simple Wheel with four spokes will be easier to affix on the Flag than the more elaborate Lotus: we shall have to consider the practical side of the question too – the National Flag will have to be made in hundreds and thousands. But the Lotus will be quite welcome, as a beautiful symbol from Nature, and the idea of Federation is exquisitely indicated by its petals. It will be quite striking when in a suitably simple and conventional form.

The above suggestions are offered for what they are worth. The present writer has discussed the matter with some of the best intellects of the country, in Bengal and outside Bengal: and the idea of vertical bands of Red, Green and Ochre or Saffron, with the three or four-spoked Wheel (or the Four or Eight Petalled White Lotus) in the central field, seemed to satisfy most people. It is now presented before the public, and before the Flag Committee appointed by the Indian National Congress; and it is done with the fervent wish and prayer that out of the endeavours of the Committee and with the co-operation and approval of the people a National Flag and a Crest be finally evolved for India which will be in perfect accordance with her great and composite culture, her noblest ideals and achievements, and her high destiny in the future.

(First published in the *Modern Review*, June 1931. The article was reprinted in *The National Flag - A Selection of Papers Cultural and Historical*, published by Mitra & Ghosh, Calcutta, 1944.)

For Further Reading

Agarwala, S. Vasudev. *The Wheel Flag of India.* Varanasi: Prithvi Prakashan, 1964.

Barraclough, E.M.C. *Flags of the World.* UK: Frederick Warne & Co, 1971.

Chatterji, Suniti Kumar. *The National Flag.* Calcutta: Mitra & Ghosh, 1944.

'Constituent Assembly of India Debates, Volume IV,' 22 July 1947. See: http://www.indiankanoon.org/doc/21455/

Crampton, William. *The World of Flags.* UK: Studio Editions Ltd., 1990.

Dutta, Bhupendranath. *Bharater Dwitiya Swadhinata Sangram.* Calcutta: Naba Bharat Prakashan, 1983 (reprint; first published 1922).

Flag Code of India, Govt. of India, Ministry of Home Affairs, New Delhi, 2002.

Furlong, W.R. and B. McCandless. *So Proudly We Hail.* Washington: Smithsonian Institution Press, 1981.

Kumar, Nagendra. *Indian National Movement.* Patna: Janaki Prakashan, 1979.

Mukherjee, Haridas and Uma Mukherjee. *'Bande Mataram' and Indian Nationalism.* Calcutta: Firma KLM, 1957.

Nair, P. Thankappan. *Indian National Songs and Symbols.* Calcutta: Firma KLM, 1987.

Neubecker, Ottfried and J.P. Brooke-Little. *Heraldry – Sources, Symbols and Meaning*. London: Tiger Books International, 1997.

Our Flag. New Delhi: Publications Division, 1989.

Singh, K.V. *Our National Flag*. New Delhi: Publications Division, 1991.

Singh, K.V. *The Indian Tricolour*. New Delhi: Rupa & Co., 2005.

Smith, Whitney. *Flags: Through the Ages and Across the World.* New York: McGraw Hill, 1975.

Specification for the National Flag of India, Indian Standards Institution, New Delhi (1968, 1977).

Talocci, Mauro. *Guide to the 'Flags of the World'.* UK: Sidgwick & Jackson, 1982.

Virmani, Arundhati. *A National Flag for India*. Ranikhet: Permanent Black, 2008.

Webb, Sophia and M.F. Stern. *Flags on Stamps*. American Topical Association, 1956.

Williams, L.N. *Fundamentals of Philately*. American Philatelic Society, 1990.

Wise, Terence. *Military Flags of the World 1618-1900*. UK: Blandford Press, 1977.

Znamierowski, Alfred. *The World of Flags*. UK: Hermes House, 2000.

Index

A
Acharya Bhavan Museum, 42
Acworth, Harry Arbuthnot, 34
Afro-Asian conference, Bandung, 1955, 108, *109*
ahimsa, 150, 151, 152
Ahluwalia, H.P.S. of Mt. Everest Expedition, 102, *102*
Aiyaswami, N., 63
Aiyer, S.A., 77
Ajanta frescos, 96
Ali, Aruna Asaf, 74, *74*
Ali, Asaf, 79
All India Congress Committee (AICC), 73
All India Flag Day (18.6.1923), 53
All India Muslim League, 61–62, 79–80, 81–82, 88
All India Sanskrit Conference, 63, 148
Amarta, 143
Ambedkar, B.R., 82–83
American National Flag, 153
Ananda Math, 44
Andaman and Nicobar Islands: Japanese siege during World War II, 77
Andrews, C.F., 63, 148
Aney, M.S., 71
Anglo-French Wars, 32
Ansari, M.A., 71
Antarctic Treaty, 104
Anthony, Frank R., 82, 89, *89*
Arabian Sea, 35
Arjuna, 9–10, 18
Army Flag Day, *127*
Aryans, 17
Asoka Chakra, 108, 124; erroneous depiction, *130*
Asian Indians in North America, postmark, *116*
Asian-Oceanic Postal Union (AOPU), 15th anniversary (1977), *108*

Asoka, 96; Dharam Chakra, 83–84; pillar, 135
Atharva Veda, 17
Atlas of the World, 31
Attlee, Clement, 81
August Kranti (August Revolution), 76, *76*
August Kranti Maidan (Gowalia Tank Maidan), 74
Aurangzeb, Emperor, 30, 150
Aurobindo, Sri, 45
Avanta, 143
Azad, Abul Kalam, 65, *65*, 71, 82

B

Babur, 11
Bahadur Shah II (1775–1862), 38
Bajaj, Seth Jamnalal, 53, *53*
Bakhuizen, Ludolf, *26*
Bande Mataram, 43–46, *44*, 80; flag, 47
Bandopadhyay, Rangalal, 56
Banerjea, Surendra Nath, *43*, 44, *44*
Barlow, Edward, 25, *26*
Barlow, Joel, 135
Basu, Bhupendra Nath, 44
Basu, Premsundar, 63
Basu, Sachindra Prasad, 44
Basu, Sris Chandra, 40
Bay of Bengal, 28
Bengal: anti-Partition movement in Bengal, 42–43, 45; Nawab of, 28
Bernier, Francois, 30
Besant, Annie, 48–49, *48*, 147
Bezwada (Vijayawada) Congress, 50
Bhagat Singh, 55, *55*
Bhagvad Gita, 10, 18
Bharater Dwitiya Swadhinater Sangram—Aprakashita Rajnaitik Itihas, 44
Bharathiyar, Subramania, 135, *135*
Bhattacharya, Vidhusekhar, 63
Bhave, Vinoba, 53, *53*
Black Flag Demonstration, 54–56
Bodhisattvas, 140
Bodi Sahib Gurudwara, 10
Border Security Force (BSF), 127, 128
Bose, Jagadish Chandra, 41, 42
Bose, Khudiram, 47, *47*
Bose, Netaji Subhas Chandra, 76–80, 97, 137; slogans *Jai Hind* and *Chalo Dilli*, 137, *137*; on matchbox, *136*; Port Blair postmark, *78*
Bose, Rajnarain, *Bridhya Hindoo-r Asha*, 40–41
Bose, Rashbehari, 57

Bourbon monarchy, restoration of, 31
Boycott Day, 43–44
Brahmacharya, 151
Brezhnev, L.I.: first state visit to India (1973), *110*; Second Visit (1980), *110*
British: colonial rulers, 11; goods, boycott, 44; flag for India, *30*
Buddha (Prince Siddhartha), 41, 140–41, 150; *Vajra-Asana*, 141, 142
Buddhism, 151
Bulgaria and India, 50th anniversary of diplomatic relations (1954–2004), *112*
Bulgaria flag, *68*, 148, 151
Bureau of Indian Standards (BIS), 130
Byzantium, 142

C
Calcutta, view, *28*
Cama, Bhikaiji Rustom, 45
Cama, Madame, 45–48, *46*, 73
Caveeshar, Sardul Singh, 71
Central Bureau of Investigation (CBI), 37
Chaturvedi, Makhan Lal, 53, *53*
Chaki, Prafulla Chandra, 47, *47*
chakra and mandala, 41
chakra flag, 84–86
chakra for the *charkha*, substitution of, 85, 153
Chandernagor, 32, *32*
Chandragupta I, *19*
Changi, 36
charkha symbol on flag, 50–51, 54, 64, 69, 72, 76, 84, 145, 152–53
Charnock, Job, 28
Chatterjee, Bankim Chandra, 44
Chatterji, Suniti Kumar, 39, 68, 89, 146–54; *The National Flag*, 60
Chauhan, Subhadra Kumari, 52, *52*, 53
Chief Inspector, Chief Inspectorate of textiles & Clothing, Kanpur, 130
Children's Day: stamp (1962), 138, *138*; India in Space, stamps (2000), *106*
Chittagong Republican Army (CRA), 59
Choudhry, Devipada, 75
Chowdary, T. Ramaswami, 69, *69*
Chowdhury, Asutosh, 44
Christians, 91
Cinderella label issued from Khadi Mondal, Calcutta, 56
Civil Disobedience movement, *52*, 63
Clive, Robert, *29*
Colachel, Battle (Kulachal, Tamil Nadu), 1741, 23–24
Colbert, Jean-Baptiste, 30
Cold War, 109
Coldstream, William, 30
colour disposition of National Flag, 67, 68–70, 72, 86, 89, 130, 144, 147–52;

communal interpretation, 148
commemorative postage stamps, 13–14
Commonwealth Day (14.3.1983), *112*
Commonwealth Heads of Government Meeting (1971), flags of member countries, *112*
Commonwealth of Nations, 112
Commonwealth Parliamentary Association, 27th Conference (1981), *112*
communal compartmentalism, 148
communal symbolism, 148
Congress, 144; Belgaum session, 148; Calcutta session, 50; Cocanada (Kakinada) session, 61; Working Committee (CWC), 65–66, 69–70, 71, 82
Conservation of Antarctic Maritime Living Resources, Convention on the (CCAMLR), 104
Constituent Assembly, 82; debates (22.7.1947), 86–92
Continental Colors (Grand Union Flag), 26
Cornwallis, Lord, *35*
Creques, Abraham, 31, *31*
Cricket World Cup, 10th (2011), *118*, 119
currency notes, showing Parliament House, *93*
Curzon, Lord, 42–43

D

D'Souza, Jerome, 90, *90*
D'Souza, Joseph Alban, 91
da Gama, Vasco, 21, *21*, 22, *22*; discovery of the sea route, *20*
Dadhichi, Maharishi, 42, *42*, 64
Dadra and Nagar Haveli, 22
Dakshin Gangotri, Antarctica, 104
Daman (Damao), 22
Dandi March, 1930, 56
de Coubertin, Pierre, *118*
de Lannoy (D'lennoy), Eustachius, 23, 24
Dead Letter Office (DLO), 52
Delhi Declaration of Six-Nation Initiative–1985 for peace and disarmament, *110*
Delhi, kingdom of, depicted on a map by Abraham Creques (1375), *31*
Desai, Bhulabhai, 79
Deshmukh, P.B., 88, *88*
detachment, 151
device on flag, 152–53
Dharma Chakra, Western Command insignia, *126*
dharmachakra, 41
dhvajapurushas, 10
Dhillon, G.S., *78*
dhvaja (standard), 17
dhvajagriha, 10
dhvajavrikshas, 10

diplomatic relations, role of flags, 112
Diu, 22
Dorji, Phu, of Mt. Everest Expedition, 102, *102*
Dravidian civilisation and culture, 18
Duarte, Teofilo, 22
Dupleix, Joseph Francois, 32; meeting the Soudhabar of the Deccan (c.1750), *32*
Durga, 42, 141
Dutch East India Company, 23
Dutt, Rajani Palme (1896–1906), 43
Dutta, Batukeshwar, 55
Dutta, Bhupendranath, 44, 46; *Bharater Dwitiya Swadhinater Sangram—Aprakashita Rajnaitik Itihas*, 46

E

Eagle of Zeus, 139–40
East India Company (EIC), 24, 25, 26, 27–28, 29; ensign (c.1616–1707), *25*; ensign (c.1707–1801), *26*; ensign (c.1801–1873), *26*; stamps issued by (1854), *29*
Eastern Shipping Corp. Ltd, 124
Edward VII, 30
Elizabeth I, Queen, 24, *24*
Emblems and Names (Prevention of Improper Use) Act, 1950, 129
European: colonialism in India, 21; flags at sea, *22*, 23; powers, 20; war flags, 10

F

federalism, 153
Festival of USSR in India, *112*
First War of Independence (1857), *37*, 38, 95; stamp to commemorate 150th anniversary, *95*
Flag Code of India 2002, 129, 131–34, 138
Flag Committee of Congress (1931), 65–70, 71, 146–54
'Flag of Convenience', 124
'Flag of the Order', 21
Flag Presentation Committee, 92
flags: and cultural ties, 116–17; at sea, 121–25; uses during state visits, 110
Fleur-de-Lis, The French Royal Flag and Ensign (1643–1790), *31*
Freedom Forty–Swaraj, postmark (16.8.1988), *101*
French: Corps in the service of Tipu Sultan, *32;* military, *31*; national flag issued by United Nations, *33*
French East India Company, 30
French Revolution, 1789, 30–31
French *Tricolore*, *39*; arrival, 30–32; worldwide impact, 32–33

G

gada of Vishnu as Hindu symbol, 148
Gajhnavi, Abdul Halim, 44

Gandabherunda: emblem of the Mysore rulers of Wodeyar dynasty, 35, *35*
Gandhi, Indira, 48, 105
Gandhi, M.K., 50–52, 56–57, 62–64, 71, 73, *74*, 80, 84–85, *84*, 132, 144–45, 148; birth centenary stamp, *82*; last journey, *131*
Gandhi, Rajiv, *72*, 113
Garuda dhvaja, 19
geographical and cultural unity, 146
George V, King, 30
Ghadge, Naik Yeshwant, *130*
Giri, V.V., 78
Goa, liberation (19.12.1961), 22, *22*
Gopalakrishnayya, D., 64
Gopi, cartoonist, *83*
Govind Das, Seth, 91
Grand Union Flag, *26*
Greeks, 139–40
Greeks Abroad, stamp 1977, *116*
green, the colour of vegetation, 130, 144, 147–52, 154
Group of 15, 7th Summit, Kuala Lumpur, 1977, *116*
Gupt, Shyam Lal 'Parshad', 135, *136*
Gupta, S.N., 82
Guptas, 19, 39, 146
Gurubaksh Singh, 79
Gyalpo, Druk, 111

H

Hafeezuddin, Begum, 62
Hansaraj, Lala, 51, 144
Hanuman, 10
Hanuman *jhanda* (Hanuman flag), 37
Har Dayal, 45
Hardikar, N.S., 65, 72, *72*
Harhama, 143
Harivamsa, 10
Hawkins, William, 24
Hayman, Francis, *29*
Hazra, Matangini, 75, *75*
Henry the Navigator, 21, *21*
Hillary, Edmund, 102
Hindavi Swarajya, 34
Hinduism, 36, 41
Hindus, 41, 48, 91, 145; and Muslims, unity, 144
Hindustan Seva Dal, 72
Hindustan Socialist Republican Association (HSRA), 55
historic consciousness of the youth, 138
Hitler, Adolf, 11

Home Rule flag, 1917, 48–49, *48*, 73
Home, Robert, *35*
house flags, 123
Hussain, Tejamul, 91
Hyder Ali, Sultan, 35

I
Imambaras, 10
Independence 25th anniversary, *132*; first postage stamp, *100*; flag logo for commemoration of 40th anniversary, *101*; flag logo for commemoration of 50th anniversary, *101*; Paying Homage to Martyrs, *136*; se-tenant stamps honouring martyrs (15.8.1998), *98*; unissued essay stamp, *100*
'India in Space, 2025', 106
Indian Antarctic Expedition, first anniversary (1983), 104, *104*
Indian Blue Ensign, 123
Indian Coast Guard, postmark celebrating 30 years, 123, *123*
Indian flag: at international sports events, 118–20; in outer space, 104–06
Indian Independence League, 80
Indian National Army (INA), 137; flag, 76–80; stamp to commemorate 25th anniversary of founding of provisional government, *77*
Indian National Congress (INC), 52, 72, 81
Indian National Flag: homage to, 92; unfurled through philately, 139–43
Indian National Flag Mission, 50
Indian National Shipowners' Association (INSA), 124, *125*
Indian National Society (INS), 40; sun flag of, 1883, *40*
Indian Navy's white ensign, 121–22, *121*
Indian Red Ensign, 123
Indian Standards Institution (ISI), 130
Indo-Bhutan friendship, 111
Indo-Soviet cooperation (1976), *112*
Indo-Soviet Shipping, 25th anniversary (1981), *112*
Indra, (lord), 41
INS Tarangini, 122
Inter-Cosmos Programme, 105
international cooperation, 110
International Day of Solidarity with the Palestinian People, stamp on (29.11.1981), *110*
international forums, uses of flags, 107–20
International Socialist Congress, Second, 1907, 45–46
international trade, 23
International Transport Workers' Federation (ITWF), 125
Iran national flag, *111*
Irwin, Lord, 90
Islam, 151
Islamic rulers of Mysore (1761–1799), 35
Ismail Sahib, Md., 99, *99*
Italy flag, *68*, 148, 151
Ivy League Yale University, 27

J

Jafar, Mir, *29*
Jagannath temple, Puri, 10, 90
Jai Hind, postmark, 99–100, *99*
Jains, 41
Jairamdas Daulatram, 71
Jallianwala Bagh massacre (1919), 53, 132, 136
Jalpati Kumar, 75
jana-desha-dharma, 143
Jauhar, Maulana Mohammad Ali, *60*, 61, *61*
Jersey multicultural spirit, stamps, *116*
Jha, Satish Prasad, 75
Jhanda Gaan, 136
Jhanda ooncha rahe hamara, 135–36
Jhandewala, 136
Jinnah, Mohammad Ali, 48, *48*, 62
Jugantar, 44
Jupiter, 140

K

Kalam, A.P.J. Abdul, 122, *122*
Kalelkar, Kaka Saheb, 65, *65*
Kalelkar, S.D., 83
Kalidasa, 10
Kalinga, 143
Kamath, Hari Vishnu, 87, 91
Kanchenjunga, 103, *103*
Kanungo, Hemchandra, 46–47
Kapidhvaja, 9–10
Kapiketana, 10
Kargil Vijay Divas, postmark, *127*
Katju, Kailashnath, 79
Kauravas, 18
Kensitas Cigarettes, *94*
Kesari, 47
Ketkar, G.V., 47
Ketu (banner), 10, 17
Khadi and Village Industries Commission, *129*
Khaliquzzaman, Chaudhry, 88, *88*
Khan, Shah Nawaz, 79, *79*
Khanda Kirpan, 36
Khandekar, H.J., 91
Kharak Singh, Baba, 63, *63*
Khare, N.B., 83
Khasi Rao, 46
Khidwai, Ameer-ud-din, 62

Khilafat movement (1919–1924), 60–61, 145, 148
Kilachand Devchand, 124
Korean War, 108
Kulinda, 143
Kumaran, Tirupur, *72*, 73, *73*
Kuru, 9
Kurukshetra, Battle, 18
Kuwait liberation, international coalition for, *110*

L
Lajpat Rai, Lala, 55, *55*
Lakshmi Bai, Queen of Jhansi (1835–1858), 37, *37*
Lalubhai Samal Das, 124
Legal Aspects, Etiquettes and Protocols, 129–34
Lehna Singh, 62
Lingaraja temple, Bhubaneswar, 10
Lodhi, Gulab Singh, 136
London Declaration, 1949, 112
lotus, an ancient Indian symbol, *41*, 153
Louis XIV, King, 30
Lucknow Residency, 94–95, *95*

M
Madhav Rao, 46–47
Madra, 143
Madurai Philatelic Bureau, *19*
Magadha, 143
Mahabharata, 9–10, 17, 140, 141
Mahadeva, 143
Mahar regiment, *126*
makardhvaja, 10
Malagasy, 11; commemorates India-USSR Inter-Cosmos space flight (1985), *105*
Malaviya, Govind, 91
Malaviya, Madan Mohan, 69, *69*, 71
Malik, S.A., 78
Malyshev, Yuri, *104*
Mandukya Upanishad, 18
Maratha(s), 34; paintings, 35; First War (1779–1782), *31*
Marichi. *See* Morriswala, Hirjibhai P.
maritime routes, 20
matchbox with the 'Bande Mataram' slogan, *45*
Mathsyaraja, 19
Mauryas, 39, 146
Meenatchi, 19
Mehta, Hansa, 92
Mehta, Mohan Singh, 91

Mexico flag, *68*, 148, 151; displayed upside down on Greek stamp, *110*, *130*
Middle East, 20
Mikhailov, M., 11
military flags, 126–28
miniature sheet (issued in 2005) commemorating the 75th anniversary of Salt Satyagraha, *57*
Mitra, Sukumar, 44
Moirang, 78
Morarjee, Narottam, 124
Morriswala, Hirjibhai P., 63
Mother Teresa, *132*
Mount Everest, conquest, 1953, 102; 50th anniversary, postmark from Darjeeling (29.5.2004), *102*; from New Zealand, *103*
Mountbatten, Lord Louis, 81–82, *94*, 96–97; London SW1 postmark (2.11.1983), *81*
mourning, position of National Flag, 131–32
Mughal Empire, 11
Muhammad, Prophet, 10
Mukherjee, H.C., 91
Musafir, Giani Gurmukh Singh, 90, *90*
Muslims, 48, 91, 99, 145

N

Nag, Kalidas, 63, 68
Nagappa, S., 91
Nagpur Flag Satyagraha, 1923, 52–57
Naidu, Sarojini, 71, 82, 90, *91*, 92
Naoroji, Dadabhai, 44, *44*, 50
Napoleon, 31, 142
National Archives of India, 98
National Flag: concept of, 11; atop Council House (Parliament Bhavan), 92–96, *93*; display with flags of other nations, *133*; international usage, 133; display on motor cars, 134, *134*; in mourning, 131–32
National Flag Day, 87
National Maritime Day, 123, *124*
nationalism, 11, 41
Nationalist Revolution, China, 57
nation-building, 14
navy blue, 130
Nazi Germany, 11
Nehru Memorial Museum and Library (NMML), 98
Nehru, Jawaharlal, 55–56, 65, 66, 67, *68*, 71, 79, 83–84, 86–88, *87*, 90, 92, *92*, *94*, 97; stamp commemorating birthday and birth centenary, *86*
Neuville, Alphonse-Marie-Adolphe de, *32*
Nishan Saheb, 36
Nivedita, Sister, 41; *Vajra* flag, 1904, 41–45, *42*, 50
Nizam of Hyderabad, 99

Non-Aligned Movement (NAM), 109; Colombo Conference (1976), *109*; Jakarta Conference (1992), *109*
Norgay, Tenzing, 102
Norman Abbey of Romney, 94

O
Olympic Games flags and stamps, 118–20; from Athens 1896 to Atlanta 1996, 100 years, *118*; India-Pakistan final match, Melbourne (1956), *118*; XVII Winter Games, Lillehammer, Norway, *118*
Omnibus Issue, 21
Order of Christ, 21
Ottoman (Turkish) empire, 60

P
Padmanabhapuram, 24
Padmini Upakhyan (The Saga of Padmini, 1858), 56
Pakistan, 99, 113; national flag, 62–63; Resolution, 62, *62*
Pal, Bipin Chandra, 45, 47
Palestine Liberation Organisation (PLO), flag, *110*
Pancha Ranga, *36*
Panchala, 143
Pandavas, 9, 18
Pandey, Chittu, 76
Pandit, Vijaya Lakshmi, *109*
Pandyan kingdom, 18–19
Panini Office, 40
Pannikkar, K.M., 82
parallelism in history, 45–48
Parthians of Central Asia, 9
partition of Bengal, 33, 42–44
Patel, Sardar Vallabhbhai, 53, *53*, 54, 65, *65*, 71, *71*, 83
Patel, Sardar Vithalbhai, 54, *54*
patriotic songs: legacy of flag, 135–38
Persia, flag, *68*, 148, 151
Philatelic exhibitions, Indian flag displayed, 120
Pillai, V.I. Muniswami, 91
pillar or *dhvaja* with a religious shrine, association of, 18
Plassey, Battle, 1757, 28, *29*
plundering of flags (*dhvajahrita*), 11
political unity of India, 39, 146
Pondicherry (Puducherry), de-facto transfer, 32, *32*
Portugal: current national flag, *21*; flags at sea, *22*
Posts and Telegraphs, Department, 100
Praetorium, 143
Pranava-Pataka, 69
Pratinidhi, 34

Praveen, S., 106
Prem Chand, 103
President of India, Standard (1950–1971), *94*
Prevention of Insults to National Honour Act, 1971, 129
Princely States, 60
Privy Purses, abolition, 60
Provincial Congress Committees, 65, 66, 67
public buildings, display of flags, 133–34
Public Flag Salutation Ceremony, 96
Purna Swaraj flag, 71, 74–75, *74*, 76, 79, 80, *80*, 83, 136; on matchbox, *136*

Q

Quit India movement, 1942, 73–76, *73*, *76*

R

Radhakrishnan, Sarvepalli, 89–90, *89*, 111, 146
Raghuvamsa, 10
Rajagopalachari, C., 52, 54, *54*, 82, *94*
Rajendra Prasad, 82–83, *82*, 86
Rajendra Singh, 75
Rajputana Rifles, 37
Ramayana, 10, 17
Ramdas, Guru, 34, *34*
Ranas of Chittor, 36
Ranjit Singh, Maharaja of Punjab, 36, *36*
Rashtrapati Bhavan, 96; central dome, postmark, *95*; set of four stamps (5.8.2011), *95;* Museum, 98
Rathyatra, Puri, *91*
Rawat, Harish C.S., 103
Ray, Nepalchandra, 63
red colour, 142, 144, 147–52, 154
Red Cross of St. George, 121
Red Ensign, 24
Red Fort (Lal Qila), *78*, 79, 92, 97–98, *98*, 137; Museum, 98
Rehabilitation in India, the Salvation Army World Series, *116*
religious beliefs and flags, 17, 84, 145
renunciation and harmlessness (*Vairagya* and *Ahimsa*), 150
Republic of Korea, stamp on Indian national flag, *109*
Retreat Ceremony (10.1.2012), *128*
Rig Veda, 10, 17
righteousness, 84
Roman Empire, Romans, 9, 139–40
Rotary International, 75th anniversary, 1980, *116*
Roy, Biren, 77
Roy, Bishwanath, 58, *58*
Roy, Raja Rammohun, 39, *39*

Royal Proclamation, 25
Roychoudhury, Debi Prasad, *75*
rupa-lakshma (symbol), 17
Russell, Oliver, 30

S

S.S. Hindostan, *28*
S.S. Loyalty, 123, *123*
Saadullah, Saiyid Mohammed, 91
Sabarmati ashram, 56
SAF Championship, Dhaka (2003), *119*
saffron or ochre colour, 130, 151, 152, 154
Saha, Panchanan: *Madame Cama–Mother of Indian Revolution*, 48
Sahgal, Prem, 77, *78*, 79
Sahu, Lakshmi Narayan, 90–91
St. George: Cross flag to commemorate 1700th anniversary of St. George, *25;* flag-mast, *27*
St. George Fort, 27, *27*
Salt Satyagraha, 56, *57*
Sanskrit College, Calcutta, *63*
Sapru, Tej Bahadur, 79
Saptarishi configuration, 48
Sarnath lion capital of Asoka, 86
Sastri, Bhimrao, 63
Savarkar, Veer Damodar, 48, 83, *83*
Scientific Committee on Antarctic Research (SCAR), 104
Scindia Steam Navigation Company, 123–24
Sen Gupta, J.M., 71
Sen, Narendranath, 44
Sen, Surjya, 59, *59*
Sepoy Mutiny. *See* First War of Independence
Shahjehan, 92
Sharma, Balkrishna, 91
Sharma, Rakesh, *104*, 105
Sheriff, Mohamed, 91
Sherpa, N.D., 103
Sherwani, T.A.K., 71
Shipping Corporation of India (SCI), 121, *121*
Shiromani Gurdwara Prabandhak Committee (SGPC), 63
Shivaji, Chhatrapati, 34, *34*
Sidwa, B.K., 91
Sidwa, R.K., 91
Sikhs, 91, 148; opposition to the *Swaraj* colours, 63
simha-langula, 18
Simon Commission, 54–55
Simon, John, 54

Sindhu, 143
Singh, Manmohan, 111; state visit to Bhutan, *111*
Singh, Ramanand, 75
Singh, Ramgovind, 75
Sinha, Satyanarayan, 91
Sinha, Umakant Prasad, 75
Sitaramayya, B. Pattabhi, 65, *65*, 66, 67, 71, 146
Siva, 141
Sivarao, D.V., 64
Smith, Whitney, 14
Sociedade de Geografia, Lisbon, Portugal, 21
South Asian Association for Regional Cooperation (SAARC), 113; commemorative stamps issued by member countries, *114*; by Bangladesh, *113*; by Bhutan, *113*; by India, *112*; by Maldives, *113*; by Nepal, *112*; by Pakistan, *114*; by Sri Lanka, *114*, *120*
South Korea, stamps issued to commemorate president's state visit (ultimately cancelled) (1983), *111*
space science and technology, 104
Srirangapatnam (Seringapatnam), siege of, 35
Straits Settlements, 80
Strekalov, Gennady, *104*
Subz Hilali Parcham, 61–62
Sudarshan chakra, 85
Sufi traditions, 35, 151
Sun Yat Sen, 57
Surat, view from the sea, *26*
Surjeet, Harkishen Singh, 55
Surya (Sun God), 17
Surya Vansi (Sun Dynasty), 36
Swadeshi flag, 43, *43*
Swadeshi movement, 41, 52
Swaraj (self-government), 64, 69
Swaraj flag, 50–59, 61, 136; and Civil Disobedience movements, 56–59, *58;* on a Cinderella label, *56*
swastika, 87
Swatantra Bharat, *52*, *86*
Syed Mohammed, 71
symbolism, 13, 64, 139

T

Tagore, Dwijendranath, 63
Tagore, Rabindranath, 34, 41, 44–45, 64, *64*, *116*, 138
tajiaghars, 10
Tamluk national government, 75
Tandon, Purushottamdas, 71
Tanzania flag: displayed upside down on Greek stamp, *110*, *130*

Tara Singh, Master, 65, *65*
Tarun Bharat, 47
Technical Development Establishment Laboratory (Stores), Kanpur, 130
Teerth, Swami Ramanand, 99
Thayin manikodi pareer, 135
Thomas Cup Championship, Malaysia (2000), *119*
Thunderbolt. *See* Vajra
Tilak Janambhumi, *48*
Tilak, Bal Gangadhar, 47, 48, *48*
Tilak Museum, Maratha and Kesari Library, Pune, 48
Tipu Sultan, 35, *35*, 36, 76
triangular flags atop a temple, 18, *18*
Tyabji, Badr-ud-Din, 83

U
Ujjal Singh, Sardar 82
Uma, 143
Union Jack, 27, *29*, 36, 48, 50, 82, 94–95, 97, 121
United East Indian Company, 23
United Nations (UN), 102, 104, 107–08; Conference for technical Cooperation between Developing Countries (TCDC) in the domain of 'Education through television'–1978, *108*; Convention on the Law of the Sea (UNCLOS), 125; flag with flags of other nations, 133, *133*; flags of member nations, *107*, *109*; flag series 1985, *109*; General Assembly (UNGA), 108, *109*; India signs charter (26.06.1945), 107, *107*; Peace Keeping Force (UNPKF), 198; Postal Administration, 108; Security Council Meeting, Addis Ababa–1972, *108*
United States of America, 26
Universal Postal Union (UPU), 108, *108*
University Science College, Calcutta, 43

V
Vairagya, 150, 151, 152
Vajra (Thunderbolt) as a symbol of National Flag, 42, 139–43
Vajrapani, 141
vajrayana astamangala, 41
Vakil, J.J., 63
Varaha-Mihira, 142
Varma, Maharaja Marthanda, 23–24
Vedas, *17*
Vellore Fort, 35–36
Vellore Mutiny, 1806, *36*
Venkayya, Pingali, 50, *50*, *51*, 144
Vereenidge Oostindische Compagnie (VOC), 23
vexillology, 14

vexillum, eagle motif of Roman Empire, 9
Viceroy's House, *94*
Victoria, Queen, 29
Vietnam, Indian flag on stamp, issued by, *120*
Vijay Divas, ceremonial flags raised on the occasion, *126*
Vincent and Grenadines, St., *130*
Vivekananda, Swami, 41
von Axter-Heudtlass, Werner and Maria, 77
vrishadhvaja, 10
Vyas, Jai Narayan, 91

W
Wadia, B.P., 48, 148
Walchand Hirachand, 124, *124*
War Memorial Arch (India Gate), 96, *97*, 98
Washington, George, 26
Waterloo, battle, 31
Wellington, Lord, 73
Wheel of Law, 84
White and Blue War Ensign, *121*
Wilkes, Mark, *27*
William I, Prince of Orange-Nassau, 23
Wodeyar dynasty, 35
World Cup Hockey Championship, Bombay (1982), *118*
World Peace Day, stamps from Bosnia-Herzegovina, *110*
World Philatelic Exhibition, Korea, 1984, *120*
World Scout Movement, 100 years (1907–2007), *116*
World War I, 47
World War II, 80, 81, 109;
    Japan's surrender (15.8.1945), *81*

Y
Yagnik, Indulal Kanhaiyalal, 47, *47*
Yajee, Sheel Bhadra, 78, *78*
Yale, Elihu, 27

Z
Zail Singh, Giani, *122*
Zoroastrians, 91
zuri-pataka, 34